SEASCAPES

SEASCAPES

TOM MACSWEENEY

MERCIER PRESS
WHAT YOU NEED TO READ

MERCIER PRESS
Cork
www. mercierpress. ie

Trade enquiries to:
Columba Mercier Distribution,
55a Spruce Avenue, Stillorgan Industrial Park, Blackrock, County Dublin

© Tom MacSweeney, 2008

ISBN: 978 1 85635 600 8

10 9 8 7 6 5 4 3 2 1

Photography © Tom MacSweeney, Catherine Twibill, Denis Murphy,
Stephanie MacSweeney, iStock.com, Stockbyte, Shannon Development,
Cork Kerry Tourism.

Mercier Press receives financial assistance from
the Arts Council/An Chomhairle Ealaíon

Printed and bound in the EU.

CONTENTS

INTRODUCTION

It was the late, great Dr John de Courcy Ireland, a man I was honoured to know as a friend, who wrote, broadcast and campaigned unceasingly for the recognition of the importance of the sea, who turned my mind to the question of why our planet is not called Ocean instead of Earth, when so much more of it is covered by water, by the seas, than by land. Perhaps it is called Earth because it is those solid pieces of land to which we humans cling and spend our lives amongst the heaving, restless, never-ending movements of the oceans.

On one of those small pieces of land, an island on the western periphery of Europe, we Irish live our lives. Our island is the first piece of solid earth against which the mighty Atlantic Ocean crashes, having rolled uncontrolled for thousands of miles across the face of the planet.

All around this island, both the twenty-six counties which constitute the Republic and the six counties that are still part of the United Kingdom, the sea accepts no boundaries upon itself, no matter what humans attempt to impose. Every minute of every hour of every day, the sea is there, a huge resource available to a small island nation. But in this Republic of Ireland, successive governments turned their backs on the sea and looked inward, rather than outward, from whence the first people to populate this island arrived – from the sea, in boats. Ireland lost the resource of its fishing industry when other European nations outmanoeuvred, out-thought and out-negotiated Irish governments.

It is the view of the fishing industry that other European nations have taken in the value of fish catches from Irish waters the equivalent of all the billions of euros in grants which Ireland has received from the European Union, earnings which have provided jobs and profitable fishing industries in those countries. Irish government decisions closed the state shipping line. It is time for a revival of Irish maritime interest and there are signs that this is occurring. Irish marine researchers and the quality of their research is respected internationally. Irish research vessels are to the fore in offshore marine exploration.

The Marine Institute and the Irish Maritime Development Office are amongst government commitments. There are commercial shipping companies, thriving ports, and a strong and growing interest in marine leisure. More needs to be done, particularly the recognition of the marine sector as a primary government role.

This book is not an account of Irish maritime history. It is a selection of the stories of a seafaring people drawn from a thousand Seascapes programmes over twenty years on RTÉ Radio 1. Selection, by its nature, cannot be comprehensive. It is based on particular people, incidents, places. The task for Seascapes, the focus of its programme approach, has been to report on the Irish marine sphere and its people, many of whom have distinguished themselves across the oceans of the world. The sea which surrounds us is not a barrier between ourselves and other nations, but a channel of opportunity, which should create pride in the distinction of being an island people and, therefore, a maritime nation.

Tom MacSweeney

1

WHAT BROUGHT ME HERE?

I'm fairly frightened, in fact I'm bloody scared! My nose is close to the bottom of a metal telephone pole. God only knows what dogs may have done around where my face is pressing against. The fleeting thought is quickly blown out my mind, just like the lights in the telephone box in front of the pole. I was in there a few minutes ago, phoning a report to the news copy desk at *The Sunday Press* back in Dublin. But then I was yelled at to 'get the hell out of there …' and I did what the British soldier told me. Why am I behind the telephone pole? It seemed the only place to go as I ran out of the box and was shouted at to 'get down'. The carefully orchestrated bravery of the 'heroes' of the celluloid world did not extend to my precarious position on the Shankill Road on the night of Saturday, 11 October 1969, a night now written indelibly on my mind.

It was somewhere between eleven o'clock and midnight and my only worry was would I live through the night. A few hours before I had gone to bed in the Wellington Park Hotel on the south side of the city, having finished a duty shift since early morning at the *Irish Press* office in Donegal Street. It hadn't been a good day; there was trouble on the streets. Women had blocked the road at Unity Flats, an indication that there might be more difficulties. There were but they came from an unexpected source – Loyalists turned on the RUC and the Shankill Road became inflamed, so the news editor back in Burgh Quay called those off-duty journalists who were on a regular rotation of duty in Belfast, to get back to work and I was sent to the trouble area. The taxi dropped me. My handkerchief was in my pocket, coated with vinegar – one of the ploys all journalists used at the time to give themselves some protection from CS gas which might be fired by the security forces at the demonstrators. It was always known in Belfast when you had been in a troubled area – coinage in your pocket was discoloured because of contact with a handkerchief.

I wasn't at the bottom of the Shankill too long when police started to advance in a line, but something happened and the word spread that an RUC man had been shot dead. His name I have not forgotten – Constable Arbuckle. It was that news which led me to follow the Landrovers and soldiers who deployed in support of the RUC along a Shankill where buildings were burning, and that originally took me into the phone box.

But it seemed that the UVF had opened fire on the troops and police, and thus the rush for cover and the warnings from the soldier. It was my first time in such a situation, under fire, and my first duty period with *The Irish Press* in Belfast. An 'innocent abroad'. I did many duty periods in Belfast and elsewhere in Northern Ireland after that, but always believed that anyone who said they were never frightened or scared were either fools or liars. Soldiers sheltered in doorways, before armoured vehicles pushed up the hill and a tough-looking Sergeant looked down at me, still lying behind the pole, 'It's the ones you don't hear that will get you mate; you can get up now …'

So, I learned, all that may be heard from a bullet is the sound from the air after it has passed and all that can be seen is a flash from a ricochet.

When that night ended, two people had been killed, a hundred arrested and nearly double that number injured.

The following morning the *Irish Press* newsdesk, preparing the Monday morning paper, sent me to Rev. Ian Paisley's church to report what he would say about the night before, which was considered extraordinary because Loyalists had opened fire on the British army. What he said does not register in my mind these many years later, because I had some difficulty in reporting it. The taxi-driver I hired to take me to the church would not go the entire way because he was Catholic. He got me as close as he reckoned safe, then gave me directions and advised me to keep my mouth shut – my accent would be a liability where I was going. It didn't give me much confidence after the night before, but more frightening would be failing to do the job to which the *Irish Press* news desk assigned you.

So I daren't take out a notebook in the church, trying to resist a mental image formulating in my mind from watching cartoons, that a large arrow would be pointing towards me indicating 'journalist – reporter'. Between this and trying to concentrate and remember what Ian Paisley would say, my arm was pulled to get my attention, and the person alongside me passed the collection, for which I hurriedly grabbed for the coinage in my pocket – quite discoloured from the night before! Then the voice alongside me hissed 'a silent collection', to which I contributed an English £5 note. A lot of money in 1969 when my weekly salary from *The Irish Press* was £21. However, it should come back – via my expenses. But it never did – somewhere in the midst of *The Irish Press* financial accounts of the time, the 'De Valera' newspaper, that particular claim for a contribution to Dr Paisley's church didn't get paid. I wondered in later years when the Irish Press Group newspapers were closed down, whether I had a justifiable claim!

My mother-in-law, a lovely West Cork woman, summed it all up when she read my by-line on the story of that Shankill night and told her daughter, my wife: 'Tell him come home from there, it's no place for a married man!'

A good idea, but in the world of journalism and the tough school that *The Irish Press* was, I wouldn't have tried that one on the newsdesk.

It was one of the experiences in a journalistic career of forty-six years which has brought me to where I am now – described as 'the voice of the marine' and known for presenting *Seascapes*, the maritime programme on RTÉ Radio, for a thousand editions.

My first job as a reporter was with the then *Cork Examiner*, in their offices on Cork's main thoroughfare – Patrick Street. That was in 1961, when luckily for me, I came straight out of school from Presentation College on the Western Road, directed to writing by what passed for career guidance in that illustrious educational establishment! In his refined, well-spoken south-city-side voice, our teacher of mathematics was asking the class what they would like to become when they left school.

To my interest in becoming an engineer, he responded with an announcement to the class: 'Mr MacSweeney wants to become and engineer ... I beg of you Mr MacSweeney, cease, desist. With your ability in mathematics, if you build a bridge it will surely collapse and I shall be known as the teacher of a mass murderer!' His suggestion that I should try to use English, perhaps as a clerk, arose from his other tutorial subject of English, for at least I was pretty good at spelling.

That was thanks to my maternal grandfather, after whom I was called Tom and with whom I lived for many years as a child. Granda Walsh was of the 'old stock'. He lived in Montenotte, regarded as one of the better parts of Cork suburbia, and he worked on the financial side with the then emerging building company, John Sisk & Son.

So he was good at figures – and did many of my mathematics lessons for me, confusing both myself and the teacher by the ways in which he worked out the answers. I was never able to do the same thing when faced with such problems in class, where Granda's benign influence was not available!

The ways of the world are strange because, years later as a marine correspondent, I would get to know one of the stalwart figures of Irish traditional boats – Hal Sisk, one of the descendants of the man who started the company for which my grandfather worked.

Granda Walsh was a great reader, who encouraged me into books and inculcated pride in spelling words correctly. If I did not know them he would teach me how to get the spelling right phonetically. To this day, I am often the resort of colleagues wishing to check the spelling of a particular word.

Granda's family connections stretched into Mid Cork, around Aherla I believe, and his wife, my grandmother, came from the Whitegate area of East Cork, on the edge of Cork harbour. At one stage they had lived in that great old part of Cork, Ninety-Eight Street, not far from St Finbarre's Cathedral. In later years I learned that a distant relation of his, Thomas Walsh, is included in the names on the monument honouring the rebels of 1798 on Cork's Grand Parade. I also learned that, on my father's side, the MacSweeneys could trace their history back to the Marsh, another legendary part of Leeside, and to one of the family who was involved in maintaining boats which very many years ago fished for salmon on the reaches of the Lee around the Mardyke, the Maltings and where the Mercy Hospital stands, close to Cork City itself.

Granda Walsh had great stories. He started work early, leaving the house by 7 a.m., and retired early. He would have a cup of tea before he turned in for the night, with a slice of buttered bread, cut into four squares by my grandmother. To get him to tell me the stories, I would take the tea and bread to his bedroom and, when he had the time, he would regale me with tales of the sea, warships and events. On occasional weekends we would walk from Montenotte down the hills to the city – we didn't have a car in those days, not many families had. Walking along Penrose and other quays, where there would be many ships tied up, he would point out the name of the ship and, beneath it, the name of where it had come from. He would discuss what it carried and, occasionally, talk to a seafarer leaning over the ship's rail.

But Granda Walsh was never at sea; his stories came from books he read and from the experience of the man who was known in the family as the one who 'walked with a roll'. In the big, mahogany glass-fronted cabinet in what was called the 'sitting-room' in Montenotte were the thinnest plates and cups, with Chinese designs on them – dragons, boats – all mixing with collections of glass and other items from around the world. These had all been brought home from seafaring trips by Granda's cousin, known as 'Tommy Leary'. He had served many years with the British Royal Navy in the early part of the twentieth century and had taken part in the Battle of Scapa Flow. He was considered unusual in family lore, the man who had done something totally different from the rest of the family. It was considered a strange thing for a family that had no connections with the ocean that he had gone to sea. Somewhere, perhaps, that tenuous connection resurfaced in another generation, for I had no connection of any kind with the sea until my career took me back from years in Dublin to Cork.

Through the *Cork Examiner*, several years, and chief reporter with the *Southern Star*, to *The Irish Press* and RTÉ, both in Belfast and Dublin, I had never owned a boat until I was assigned back to Cork in the 1970s as RTÉ's first regional correspondent. While I was serving as Munster correspondent, an old fisherman in Kinsale told me: 'Down here you should have a boat.' So it was that, pushing thirty, I first learned to swim and took an adult training course on National 18 dinghies at Monkstown Bay Sailing Club, of which I am still a member, and where, in the 1980s, I came to live close to Cork harbour.

Such is what brought me to the sea and to pestering RTÉ to start a marine programme, because I came to the belief that the sea was essential to 'an island nation'.

2

'THIS ISLAND NATION'

People have lived in the coastal regions of Ireland for more than 9,000 years. It would be reasonable to expect that from such a tradition the politicians who lead our nation would have a pride in its maritime tradition. That they do not disgusts and frustrates me.

Irish politicians destroyed the shipping and fishing industries. It is a legacy of which they should be ashamed. Irish Shipping, the state company, is an example of how politicians do not deserve to be trusted. The fishing industry is another.

I sat opposite a senior politician with a long family tradition who waxed lyrical about what his family had done for the state. It was with a deep sense of disgust that I listened to him say – 'I'm the minister now for fish and ships, but we all have to suffer a little'.

He had been appointed Minister for the Marine, but thought so little of the ministry that he considered it a 'minor appointment' in the cabinet and his hope was to get promotion 'to a more senior posting'. As I listened to him I felt a sense of revulsion that this well-suited man with his home in Dublin was the one on whom fishermen, working in one of the most difficult and dangerous occupations imaginable, would be depending to oversee state commitment to their industry. He was a failure as Minister for the Marine and others have not been much better. The Irish government so disregards the marine that there is now not even a single department which has the word 'marine' within its title.

This is the government attitude towards the marine sphere in a nation which has produced Admiral Barry of Wexford, who created the American navy; Admiral William Brown of Foxford, who created the Argentinian navy; John Holland, who invented the submarine; and Arctic explorers like Tom Crean and Francis Leopold McClintock. These men and others like them do not merit the same mention in Irish history as those figures who were landbound.

In the Second World War the nation faced isolation and starvation. Irish Shipping was established by the government, and seafarers sailed vessels often ill-suited to the oceans they crossed, in order to provide the people with essential fuel and food supplies. They had no protection, trusting in the tricolour and the word Eire painted on the sides of the vessels. 149 died when this did not deter the warring factions, who ignored neutrality and sank thirteen Irish vessels. The company continued operating until the 1980s, when the government put it into liquidation because of the failures of on-shore management. It was the first state company to be liquidated and seafarers were left without jobs; several, who had served during the war were denied their pensions.

Such was the reward of the state to those who had served it loyally.

The fishing industry was sold out, some would say betrayed, by the country's most senior politicians and civil servants when they negotiated Irish membership of the then Common Market, now EU, in the 1960s and 1970s. They gave away rights to the most lucrative, valuable fishing waters in Western Europe, leaving Irish fishermen with a small percentage of entitlement to fish in their own waters.

'The French saw them coming and made mincemeat of them,' Lorcan Ó Cinnéide of the Irish Fish Producers' Organisation told me. 'The French insisted on common waters, community ownership. They didn't try to tell Irish farmers that French fishermen should have rights to Irish fields, but the government civil servants and politicians allowed them to gain rights over Irish waters.'

Billions of euro and hundreds of jobs in what should have been a viable fishing industry were lost because of the stupidity and ignorance of politicians. Those on the negotiating team who objected to this were sent home. The level of incompetence was appalling. Those responsible should have been held accountable. Instead it was the fishermen and the fishing industry who have suffered ever since. The politicians and the civil servants said they were gaining benefits for Irish farming and had to make concessions, so fishing rights were conceded. On both issues they erred. Ireland has contributed as much to the EU in the value of fish taken from its waters by other Community countries as it has gained in all the grants received from the EU.

It disappoints me that in an island nation, our historic perception does not emphasise maritime tradition to the same extent as inland aspects of our heritage. The history of the Irish people stems from those who arrived first on our shores to establish communities. There is some disagreement amongst historians as to the date at which a land bridge last connected

Ireland and Britain, but it is believed that such a connection did not survive beyond 10,000 years ago. Archaeological records indicate that the first inhabitants of Ireland arrived after the last Ice Age, some 9,000 years ago in the Mesolithic period. This is based on artefacts such as stone tools and domestic debris found in coastal areas, on lake shores and riverbanks. These facts indicate that the first people to arrive in Ireland came from the sea, crossed open water and, to do so, used boats. The Mesolithic travellers who first arrived on Irish shores founded an island nation which relied on the bounties provided by the sea and so they established their settlements close to the coast. Today our major cities are all based on the coast.

They were our forbears in an 'island nation', but modern-day politicians have failed to realise the value of the sea. The maritime sphere has been treated dismissively by the state, by politicians and civil servants who turned their backs on the sea and looked inwards, neglecting the sea and the bounty it offers.

Beautiful Brandon Creek on the Kerry coastline is where St Brendan and his crew of monks are believed to have departed from on their voyages in the sixth century, during which they may have discovered America long before Columbus. There I pondered why successive Irish governments have failed to capitalise on the nation's maritime potential. To live close to the sea, to seek to understand and appreciate it, is to understand the reason for life itself and how it survives on an island nation.

An 'island nation' – words I have spoken every week for sixteen years on national radio, words that I now hear repeated as they become part of everyday language in Ireland, words that should hold a pride in reflecting the maritime history, culture and tradition of an island on the western extremity of Europe.

Boats, ships, the sea, the coast, have been vital, pivotal in the lives of the coastal people who were the forefathers of Ireland. Their descendants, the Irish of successive generations, have made a remarkable contribution to the maritime history of the world. There are records of Irish seafarers involved in fighting the Roman empire, of Irish ships developing foreign trade in the Middle Ages, of Irish sailors being involved in the exploration of the Antarctic. Irishmen developed the submarine and the marine turbine engine and led the formation of navies in several countries of the world.

3

IGNORING OUR ISLAND BIRTHRIGHT

One of the greatest failings of Irish people, in my view, is to appreciate, to understand, to relish, respect and accept that they are an island people. This is particularly evident amongst those who should give leadership, amongst whom I include leaders of state, business and commerce, church, industry and community. The continuous concentration on the creation of a 'knowledge' economy is irritating when there is no balance in appreciation shown of the maritime resources which those of 'knowledge' should be actively promoting in an island economy. There is a role for advancing the nation in the 'knowledge' economy – modern communications cannot be ignored – but to exclude the maritime sphere is to ignore a vital aspect of our nation. We are a small island on the periphery of Europe, yet we hold huge marine resources because of our island position. Why is the marine sector so ignored?

The development of the Marine Institute in County Galway is cited as an example of the state's commitment in recent years and this has been positive, but the marine is still far too much overlooked at national level. There is no Department of the Marine; it was abolished by the government and various aspects of its work placed in several different departments. That underlines the attitude at cabinet level that the marine is not a post of importance and not a senior portfolio, a denial of our roots of being an island people.

They may not like it, they may wish to deny their birthright, but everybody born in Ireland has been given the place in life of being an islander. Were that realisation to be appreciated, this country could have a strong economy based on its own natural resources and not be dependent on foreign investment in industries for which we do not have any such natural resources. Those are the industries that can be removed from Ireland on the decision of multinational shareholders and managements.

Our marine resources could not be so removed.

4

SEASCAPES BECOMES A REALITY

Why our government has so neglected the marine has caused me concern and thought for many years. When I was assigned to Cork, back to my home place, in 1972 to become RTÉ's first regional correspondent, I was given the task of developing a system of regional coverage for radio and television news. My base was the RTÉ studios on Union Quay in Cork, in a building shared with the Cork School of Music. It had an imposing entrance, but beyond that façade not a lot of space. A stairs wound up from an empty hallway to a reception area and a corridor, off which there were four offices and two restrooms – one being needed for men and the other for women, in those days of official separation of the sexes. There was a tape and disc library, double sound-proofing doors which led to a large studio, two studio control rooms, a small studio known as the 'talks' studio and a technical control room.

I was given a desk in a room shared with the secretary to the producers of programmes. News did not appear to have a lot of priority. The studio technical boss at the time told me that it only opened from 9 a.m. to 6 p.m., with lunch from 1 to 2 p.m., so that news reports sent into bulletins at 8 and 9 a.m., 1.30 and 6.30 p.m., which were then the bulletin times on radio – there was no other channel – would present difficulties. Television was not of particular interest to him as this was a 'radio studio'. There was a contract television cameraman and sound recordist. Television reports would have to be sent to Dublin by train, the last suitable scheduled service of which was 2.30 p.m., otherwise they would have to be driven to Montrose in Dublin.

Such were the early challenges of news coverage in the provinces, but they were met and gradually technical development overcame the difficulties and change came at a rapid pace, to the stage where now there is instant replay from Cork and reception in Dublin, live inserts and numerous television and radio channels.

But the constant for me has been the sea and the coastline, so much of it all around the Munster region which was my 'beat' and so many news stories associated with the sea. Not that every superior of mine or executive in RTÉ appreciated the importance I placed on maritime stories. At one of the regular meetings with staff, I was reproached because, this executive example of what later became called 'human relations' told me, 'too many of your stories are watery'. I reminded him that five of the six counties which I covered bordered on the sea, that there was a huge coastline and, away from his base of Dublin, people actually lived and worked in the coastal areas and created stories, but he reflected an inward-looking mind.

Fortunately, he did not hold much sway in editorial affairs and I was lucky that another Corkman, whom I had known first as a reporter, then presenter and editor in RTÉ News, was appointed controller of RTÉ Radio. He was Kevin Healy, who had begun his journalistic career in the then *Cork Examiner*, as I had myself. I approached Kevin with the idea for a programme on RTÉ Radio 1 which would cover the marine sphere – the shipping and fishing industries, and the marine environment generally, including leisure aspects. I proposed that it would develop regular contacts with the maritime agencies and also look back at our maritime history, develop an interest amongst listeners in marine activities and, as well as being attractive to those who were involved in marine affairs, would appeal to those who might know nothing about the sea but would be interested in what we reported.

It was not going to be a concept easy to sell, or easy to accept. I knew that. The sea, water, boats – all were images, more suited perhaps to television than radio. I told Kevin I was convinced I could make it work and pledged that it would not cost a lot of money. I would do it for no extra cost, would not ask to be paid for it, and would regard it as part of my duties and included in my RTÉ salary. It would be practically cost-neutral in the description which the financial side likes to hear. Kevin thought it over and, with summer approaching in 1989, gave me approval for a fifteen-minute programme on Friday nights, but for the 'summer schedule' only, meaning that the programme would end its run in September.

Fortunately, listener reaction has been such that it has never come off the air since. It has been broadcast each week and, though shuffled around in the schedule – moved to different days and times – it has continued to have a loyal audience that has followed it around and continued to increase. Over the years we have developed one of the leading web pages on the RTÉ site, a podcast and an early morning repeat of the programme, as well as a teletext news service on RTÉ television's AERTEL.

In 1997, what seemed to me the next logical step in my career happened when RTÉ accepted my personal campaign for appointment as marine correspondent. I made the case that RTÉ had an agriculture correspondent, an industrial correspondent, an economics correspondent, a religious correspondent, and several regional correspondents, so why should there not be a marine correspondent. This was accepted and I became RTÉ's first marine correspondent and the only journalist in the national media sector exclusively devoted to maritime matters. *Seascapes* remained as part of my duties. Since I was first sent to Cork I had learned to sail, owned boats and was told by colleagues that I now had both a job and a hobby.

5

IGNORING OUR
MARITIME HISTORY

As I have previously mentioned, great Irish seafarers have been ignored officially, though not by their local communities, thankfully. But often it has been those with an interest in the maritime sphere who have forced the government to give attention to our maritime historical figures.

William Brown, founder of the Argentine navy, is one example of this. It was only the determination of the people of Foxford in County Mayo and their liaison with the Argentinian authorities, that forced – some would say shamed – the Irish government into honouring this great mariner.

Born in Foxford in 1777, Brown was taken to Philadelphia at the age of nine and, when his father died, went to sea as a cabin boy, working his way over the years to become a ship's captain. This role brought him to Buenos Aires in 1812, where he spent two years trading. In 1814, at the government's request, he fitted out a squadron to fight the Spanish navy, then in mastery of the South American seas and opposed to the Argentinians' desire to control their own affairs. In his first battle he had a fleet formed of three old whaling ships, with which he defeated the Spanish and later set up the navy of the infant Republic of the Argentine. There were ups-and-downs in his relationship with the politicians in later years, but the Irishman was regularly called on for help. This included a war with Brazil and another with Uruguay in 1852, when he was over sixty years of age and during which he destroyed the naval attachment commanded by Garibaldi, who was later to win fame in Italy.

Brown kept the Argentine navy flag flying proudly for some forty years and is a hero to the Argentine people, where everything from streets to football clubs, and even an Antarctic research station, are named after him. There is a monument to him in Buenos Aires and he is commemorated by the Argentinian navy in a number of ways, none more so than through the Instituto Nacional Browniano, an institution dedicated to naval history and named in his honour. He died in 1857 and is buried in Buenos Aires. After long campaigning by his admirers in Foxford, he was formally recognised at a national ceremony held in Dublin on 22 June 2007.

He was just one of many men who have not been adequately recognised nationally and about whom little is taught in the history lessons in our schools.

First United States Navy Commodore John Barry

On the foreshore in Wexford is a memorial to Commodore John Barry, son of Catherine and John Barry, who hailed from Tacumshane. To stand there and look outwards to the sea, noting the words on the memorial, is to marvel at how boys leaving their homes at young ages could rise to such heights.

John Barry was born in 1745 and was another who went to sea at a very young age in the only position he could get – as a cabin boy. For a young lad it was tough work, at nearly everyone's beck and call, carrying, fetching; the conditions often not good and the food not great. He was often wet, cold, hungry, exhausted. On a voyage to New England he decided to stay there and try to improve his life, which decision took him to Philadelphia, where he worked his way through the seafaring ranks, as had William Brown. He also became captain of a merchant ship, at which he prospered and became wealthy, a figure of importance in his adopted country.

When the American Revolution broke out, he offered his services to the American Congress and, in February 1776, he was appointed to command a brig with sixteen 4-pounder guns called the *Lexington*. In this he carried out the first-ever capture of a ship by the American navy when he took the British tender, *Edward*, off the Virginian coast in April of that year. In 1777 he led four boats to capture an English man-of-war in what was described as a 'courageous action' on the Delaware River. He was made commander of the thirty-two-gun *Raleigh*, but lost her to the fifty-gun *Experiment*, when he had to run her ashore. The vessel was taken by the British navy and ever since the name has been retained by them. But Barry was not beaten and had other successful actions, being given the frigate *Alliance* with thirty-two guns and in which he took the first representative of the United States to the court of Versailles in France in 1781. He was severely wounded on the return voyage in a battle with the British. However, he captured two of the British vessels and brought them back to America.

His achievements and several successes led to the British trying to persuade him to join them, which he refused, and, after hostilities ceased, he commanded the frigate *United States*.

In the re-organisation of the US navy, he was appointed its first commodore, which position he held until his death on 13 September 1803 in Philadelphia. His name is remembered on ships of the US navy.

Wind force Beaufort

'Force 7 due', warns the met office report, and that tells me, as my boat swings at anchor in West Cork, that it's going to become pretty windy and I had better ensure the anchor is well dug in or, if the wind direction looks like there might be a difficult night ahead, move somewhere else if that is possible. Wind force is an essential piece of information at sea and it is the Beaufort scale which decides the different levels and the wind speed accorded to them. It was Francis Beaufort from Navan in County Meath, the son of a rector, who devised the system and was yet another young Irish boy who went to sea as a cabin boy, when he joined the British navy at the age of thirteen. He was just sixteen when he began to keep records and make comments about the weather he was experiencing and continued to maintain these until his death in 1857.

It was in 1805 that he was given his first command of a ship, the *HMS Woolwich,* in which he was ordered to carry out a hydrographic survey of the Rio de la Plata area of South America. It is conceivable that he was around those waters while William Brown was not that far away. While on this voyage he began developing what he called his 'Wind Force Scale and Weather Notation Coding'. He was wounded in 1812 while on a hydrographic survey in the eastern Mediterranean, when struck in the groin by a musket ball after rescuing a shore party;

this ended his sea-going career. In 1829 he was appointed Hydrographer to the Admiralty and in 1838 the Beaufort Wind Scale was adopted by the British navy and is still used in all maritime wind observations to this day. He was promoted to Rear Admiral in 1846 and only retired when he reached the great age of 81, having made a huge contribution in the marine sphere.

HALPIN AND THE *GREAT EASTERN*

When I first saw photographs of the *Great Eastern* they made a huge impression on me. At the time of its building it was the biggest ship in the world and remains a legendary story in world maritime affairs – and it was commanded by an Irishman. A Wicklow man, born on 17 March 1836, Robert Halpin was another who went to sea at a very young age – just ten years old – but by the age of twenty-two he was master of a steamship. In 1869 he became master of the *Great Eastern*, which had six masts, carried 6,500 square yards of sail and had two fifty-eight-foot paddle wheels. The original intention had been that she would be a passenger vessel, but this proved to be a complete failure, and when Halpin took over she was a cable ship assigned to lay the first transatlantic cables. Under his command she laid 26,000 miles of cables, linking Brazil with Europe, Australia with New Zealand and then the Dutch East Indies, Brest with Newfoundland, and Bombay with Aden and Suez, huge tasks in times when there was less technical knowledge than today.

Artefacts from the *Great Eastern* and one of Halpin's uniforms are in the possession of the Maritime Institute of Ireland.

THE CHRISTIAN BROTHER WHO TOOK WAR UNDER THE SEA

On the northside of Cork there is a school which stands high over the city and relishes its reputation as an institution where Irish is the main language of tuition; it has also produced great hurling teams and some of the stars of the sport. It is a school of the Christian Brothers, though nowadays it is lay teachers who are the dominant force, as the religious life has failed to attract sufficient numbers. In the 1860s it was home to a brother who was not much good at teaching, but who was to use a water pool in the school grounds to develop his ideas on what would become one of the most formidable, dangerous killing machines in war: the submarine.

John Philip Holland was born in Liscannor in County Clare in 1841, but it is only in recent years that the town has claimed him as their own. He was not particularly successful as a teacher, nor that happy as a Christian Brother, and so left the religious life which he had joined at the age of seventeen.

He sailed to America in 1873 and, in Boston, met up with Irish-Americans who supported the Fenians. He received funding for his first attempt at devising a submarine, which became famous as the *Fenian Ram*. It was powered by an internal combustion engine, had a single missile tube and was successful in its trials. But it never sailed in combat and it was fifteen years before the US navy bought his sixth design in 1900, judged to be the world's first successful submarine.

Another Irish impact on world maritime history.

POLAR EXPLORERS

Others who made their mark on the maritime world were the Irish polar explorers, Tom Crean of Annascaul in County

Kerry (whom I first learned about when I called into the South Pole Inn, Annascaul, County Kerry, which he owned), Ernest Shackleton, born in Kilkea, in the green, rolling hills of Kildare, and Francis Leopold McClintock, known as 'The Arctic Fox', born in Dundalk in 1819, one of the leading Antarctic explorers in the Victorian era, who discovered the fate of the lost Franklin expedition.

BY STEAMSHIP TO AMERICA

On the riverfront near Passage West in County Cork is an artefact from the *Sirius*, part of the engine of the vessel which reached New York in April 1838, the first scheduled passenger-carrying steamer to arrive from what was called the 'Old World' to the 'New'. 'I am the proudest man in the world,' the man in command, Lt Richard Roberts, RN, pronounced himself. He was born overlooking Passage West in Cork harbour from where the *Sirius* started her voyage. It was a difficult one, but when she reached New York she had ushered in the beginning of a new era in transatlantic voyaging, a new era in transport.

THE TANNER WHO FOUNDED THE URUGUAYAN NAVY

To these names should be added that of Peter Campbell, originally a tanner's apprentice, who was to found the Uruguayan navy. Campbell had first arrived in the River Plate area as an enlisted man with the British army, which had invaded Buenos Aires but failed in its campaign and withdrew. He slipped the leash of the retiring forces and stayed to join the patriot ranks, becoming legendary as a guerrilla leader against the Spanish. He began putting a squadron of river vessels together to support the fight for independence. On 21 August 1818, he became the first naval commander of the guerrilla fleet and fought against the Paraguayans. Later defeated, his life was spared out of respect for his fighting prowess and he returned to his trade as a tanner. He is honoured in Uruguay as the founder of their navy and is interred in Montevideo.

From these men and what they achieved – and there are many others who could be named – it is fair to contend that our history has ignored huge maritime contributions, not only in Ireland, but across the world.

6

LANDING THE MUNSTER FUSILIERS AT GALLIPOLI

There was one great man I interviewed who told me I had a 'soft' job and that if he had been lucky enough to get one like it, he would never have gone to sea. It was unlikely that he would have done, as there was no RTÉ Radio at the time he went to sea and if he had obtained a 'soft' job, he would not have lived history, nor achieved a unique position as a seafarer.

There is sometimes a moment when during a recording you realise with a feeling of excitement that you are getting a really good interview, one that you will remember. So it was in Waterford when I met Captain Richard Farrell. He was ninety-five at the time, but he had a clinically accurate memory and a jocular attitude to life that brought a smile to his face and a chuckle when he told his story. But the story he told me was far from enjoyable, for he had been at the core of one of the bloodiest battles in the history of warfare.

In the twentieth century, there were two world wars. The first, from 1914 to 1918, involved trench warfare and battles in which there was huge loss of life and appalling injuries and maiming. One of the greatest horrors was at Gallipoli, known mostly to the present generation perhaps through the film of the same name and anti-war songs which emanated from it, such as the story told in the Australian 'Waltzing Matilda', because the Aussies took massive casualties.

The Dardanelles are an important waterway, a passage connecting the Bosporus to the Black Sea and the Mediterranean. There had been two previous battles of the Dardanelles – one in 1656, when Venice and the Knights of Malta fought against the Ottoman empire, and one in 1807 during the Russo-Turkish War. Neither were as bloody as the battle which was fought in 1915 and 1916. It began when Russia and Britain declared war on the Ottoman Turkish Empire, to which Germany had provided warships and which had closed the Dardanelles to allied shipping in October 1914. When the Turks attacked Russia, it appealed to Britain for help. With stalemate on the Western Front and the Dardanelles blocked off, Britain decided to force a way through the Dardanelles, to enable relief convoys to get through and reach Russia, a plan devised by the then First Lord of the Admiralty in Britain, Winston Churchill.

Gallipoli is a Turkish seaport on the northeastern extremity of the Dardanelles. Steep sides dominate the area and it was extremely difficult to capture. What was to become a ten-month battle of attrition began on 19 February 1915, with an unsuccessful naval assault. In March, the British, supported by Australia and New Zealand, formed an invasion force of 70,000, but the campaign was a disaster and many thousands of soldiers died. Captain Richard Farrell, yet another Irishman who went to sea at a young age, sailed into Suvla Bay with the guns of the Turkish army raining shells down on the ships and the soldiers trying to land on the beaches. It was a chilling scene of carnage, dead and wounded lying on the beaches and in the water, the sound of exploding shells, gushes of sand and water blown up, men screaming from their wounds, dying – the water's edge tinted crimson from their blood.

Farrell wound up there as captain of one of the troop ships. When I met him in Waterford, he was the only Irishman living who had the unique qualification of holding a master's foreign seagoing certificate for the real, old square-riggers, the original tall ships, the ones now celebrated through the ships surviving today. His experience was tough and he rounded that forbidding landmark, Cape Horn, in them:

'The conditions in those sailing ships were terrible going around Cape Horn. They had only a freeboard [the distance between the sea and the top of the bulwark on the deck] of about six feet and in any kind of a sea, with high waves, they were like submarines. When the big seas came over and you were pulling the braces on the yards to control the sails, it was awful. You had to jump back to grab a line until the sea had gone off the deck again. We had lifelines rigged around just to hold onto, which would save your life that you wouldn't be swept overboard, that you could hold on and stay on the ship.

'I went around Cape Horn under sail twice. The first time I was an able seaman in a four-masted barque called the *Georgian Hill* out of Glasgow. Then my second time I was second mate of a barque called *Killoran*. That ship carried about 45,000 sq. feet of canvas, a lot of canvas. These ships were mostly in the Australian trades. We were carrying bricks made of coal dust and cement, which we discharged in England and went in ballast back to Australia and then loaded wheat. The longest time at sea in one go aboard them, without getting home, was 145 days on board.'

The 'Captain', as he was known to many in Waterford, where he had served as harbour master and a pilot, lived history and, in the interview, described it. His experiences were what books have been written and films made about:

'The conditions were blooming poor. The food was not good. It was mostly all salted beef and pork, kept in casks on deck and when they were opened up, the smell of the meat would nearly kill you it was so awful. Some of it was gone blue and the cooks would have to cut off those pieces before you could eat it.'

The pay wasn't great either. Even in those times, when money was worth a lot more, for the tough life of serving on a tall ship an able seaman was only paid £5 a month. He got his food aboard, but it wasn't very good.

Captain Farrell told me that he went to sea when he was fifteen and that he was at sea during the war. I thought that he meant the Second World War, but it was the First, his experience of life went so far back. He told me how his ship had sailed from Australia and taken the First Australian Light Horse to Gallipoli at the early stages of preparation for the landing. Following that, his ship was assigned to take the Munster Fusiliers to Gallipoli. It was an Irish infantry regiment of the British army, raised and garrisoned in Ireland. In March 1915 the regiment sailed for the Dardanelles, with twenty-eight officers and 1,002 other ranks. It suffered massive casualties at Gallipoli. Captain Farrell told me:

'When we took the Munster Fusiliers aboard, they were mostly Irish boys, some of them green as grass, as young as eighteen. One young fellow said to me one day when the crew were washing down the decks with salt water: "Is that water fit to drink?" He didn't even know the difference in salt water.

'We went into Suvla Bay and there were forty-five ships in convoy and we were placed in a semi-circle all around Suvla Bay and the Turks were on the top of the hill firing down on the beach where we were landing the Munster Fusiliers there on the beach and the poor devils, they were no sooner on the beach than they were scattered, some killed, others maimed. They were being brought back out to a big hospital ship that was moored there, all blood covered and with blood-soaked bandages.

'There was a big difference between what was happening to them and the officers who were in charge of directing the battle, I can tell you. I remember that a big incident for the officers who were out on big ships in the bay was that a shell came down and it went through the saloon of a ship called the *Shropshire* and it broke the grand piano and that annoyed them and it was a great item of discussion amongst the fellows on the ships.'

Captain Farrell's ship was in that 'hell of Suvla Bay' for about a month, in that 'awful situation', and was then used to take off injured survivors.

In his mind's eyes, as he spoke to me, pictures of that experience were whirling around, but he was young at the time and able to withstand what would nowadays require counselling and treatment for the pressure and stress suffered.

There was no such help then and Captain Farrell sailed on in his seagoing career and into the Second World War.

'For a young fellow especially, you don't feel fear as much as later in life, but there was the threat from German submarines when you were at sea, that you would not know when one would blow you up and we never took our clothes off. We slept in them as we sailed between ports in case we were torpedoed. It would be a harrowing time for anyone who had any sense, but I suppose we didn't have too much of that, because we were young and it was all excitement.'

In the 1940s, his uncle was harbour master in Waterford and 'on the point of retirement'. Richard Farrell, now with his captain's rank, arrived there knowing 'that there was the prospect of a job'. His uncle announced his retirement 'and I had to go before the harbour commissioners, but I got the job on which they had to take a vote and every vote that was going for the job I got, except one and I won't say why that was.'

He worked on as harbour master until his retirement, having had huge experiences at sea, a man who saw and was involved in the making of history and one of the best interviewees I have had the satisfaction of recording.

He was a man who loved the sea, but had a strong belief that Irish people did not generally respect the seafarer 'even though they depend on him, they need him so much to get what they need to live. Look at how much we depend on the sea for exports and imports.'

If Captain Richard Farrell had one grievance, it was that lack of recognition of the sailor:

'There has never been enough recognition for the seafarers in Ireland. Very few people in Ireland had any regard for the sailors and still don't. They didn't seem to look upon seafaring as a proper kind of job. It was looked upon as if the fool of the family was the one who went to sea, but I had a happy life and look back on the sea that it gave me a good life. I enjoyed very much my time at sea.'

The interviewer often tries to end an interview like this with the question to the interviewee: 'Would you ever have changed anything about your life?'

To which he chuckled and answered, as I will always remember: 'I would not have gone to sea at all. I'd have taken up a job in the bank, a safe job, a soft one. Going to sea was like a tinker's job: you were here today and somewhere else tomorrow. I would have had a soft job like you fellows have, like you – now *you* have a good, soft job!'

7

THE ONLY SUBMARINE COMMANDER TO SURVIVE AN ENTIRE WAR

Oranmore Castle stands on the edge of Galway Bay, a short distance from the village of the same name which most people by-pass on the road into Galway. The village itself is home to a few lovely restaurants and attractive pubs, places which a journalist tends to find, for various reasons, but oft-quoted for 'meeting a contact'. It's a place with a long and proud history, of which Oranmore Castle, a twelfth century Norman keep, is very much a part.

On the road south out of Oranmore, a right turn presents a picture post card vision of Rinville, as the road descends past a lovely park to the sea. There the boats of Galway Bay Sailing Club, itself perched on the promontory, lie at their moorings throughout the summer, bows swinging with the tide to face towards the Aran Islands, as they tug at their anchoring ropes, dancing in anticipation of racing down the bay. Southwards across the headlands and the islands is Kinvara, where the famous Galway hookers hold sway, the elite of the western sailing world, about which more later.

At Oranmore Castle lives a man who is unique in maritime

history – the only British submarine commander to start and finish the Second World War alive. A man who tried three times to sail around the world and was stopped by a hurricane, polar ice and a great white shark!

I walk past the iron gate along the driveway, see a figure across the garden and meet a sprightly man who conveys inner confidence, yet with an enchanting self-deprecation of what he has achieved.

'Submarines,' he says, 'the reality was a lot different to what it appeared in the films. When we opened the hatch after days of men confined inside a metal tube underwater, the smell was appalling. It was nauseous as it poured out and we gulped fresh air. Don't be deceived by the portrayal in the films. It was a lot different I can tell you.'

And he could.

Commander Bill King is a legend, descended, he says, from the medieval Emperor Charlemagne, which, he says, entitles his family to look on the present British royal family as late arrivals on the royalty scene!

I have been told by his daughter, Leonie, who lives in the castle with him, that Bill is deaf in one ear and to address questions to his left-hand side. His first hearing problem was caused by a battleship! He is easy to talk to and we walk through a pleasant, lived-in kitchen, which has that sense of being the heart of house, past a conservatory and into the main hall of the keep with a huge fireplace, where Bill chuckles with humour as he recalls entertainment, parties and good times. The castle seems just right as the place where Bill King would live.

He bought it with his wife, Anita for £200 in 1946, after both of them had survived the Second World War, he on submarine service and she as an ambulance driver in France, for which she was awarded the French *Croix de Guerre*.

It took many years of effort, time and expense to re-roof the castle and Bill discovered that an ancestor of his had been in it when it was stormed by Oliver Cromwell in 1652.

Extraordinarily, Anita had family connections with two men who had led their nations during the war and who had 'crossed swords' in words. Her godfather was Eamon de Valera and she was a cousin of British premier, Winston Churchill. Even stranger, her father was a good friend of the man who has become something of de Valera's nemesis – Michael Collins.

Bill and Anita bought Oranmore Castle the year they married, a wedding that presented its own difficulties because Anita was Catholic and Bill a Protestant, not the easiest of religious relationships at a time when the Catholic Church did not favour such liaisons. However, like many other situations he faced in life, it did not stop him.

My interest in Bill King derived from hearing the stories about his sailing prowess and the legendary yacht, *Galway Blazer*. So I was introduced to him first at a hotel in Salthill in Galway and later met him at his home, recording and filming his story both for *Seascapes* on radio and *Nationwide* on RTÉ 1.

Bill was born in Hampshire in England in 1910. His father, William, was killed in the First World War when a shell hit his position in the trenches. So his mother, Georgina, took him to Scotland and the home of her parents near Oban and that was, perhaps, the defining moment of his life, for his grandmother had a boat.

'It was a gaff cutter, fifty tons and had five paid hands. It was called *Imatra* and there were great times on it. I loved the boat and being on the water. So I started sailing at the age of seven with my grandmother. Now how many young boys get a chance like that!'

But he also had to go to school and there things were not great.

'It was frightful. The headmaster flogged us and I got beaten a few times, but it was a saving grace to be in the choir and you even got a boiled egg in the mornings for that.'

It wasn't a great educational experience but in accordance with the family military tradition and his love of water, Bill enrolled in the Royal Naval College in Dartmouth at the age of fourteen. Three years later, in 1927, he progressed from the 'ferocious training experience of Dartmouth' to sail as a cadet officer aboard *HMS Nelson* and suffered his first physical setback.

She was the Royal Navy's newest battleship and Bill was sent to the crow's nest up on the mast to be a spotter as the ship fired a broadside from its nine 16-inch guns. He hadn't been issued with any ear protectors – there weren't such things in those days – and he was partially deafened. His hearing was never the same. But there was no question of deafness claims against the authorities then. It was a case of suffer on and serve the navy.

His next ship was *HMS Resolution*, but Bill was adventurous and 'volunteered' for submarines. As he recounts that decision he shakes his head, still in some wonderment as to why he decided to serve below the surface rather than above it.

'I was sent to China and the Philippines and then a war was coming and it started in 1939.'

By this time Bill had risen to the rank of commander of the submarine, *Snapper*:

'We were all relatively young. I was twenty-nine and in charge and it was a mixture of responsibility, daring, being adventurous but there were also times of fear and worry, particularly because you were concerned for your men whom you were responsible for taking into danger. Submarines were uncomfortable, they were cramped, there wasn't much room, everyone lived close together. Can you imagine the smells? Dampness underwater, clammy, sweat mixing with cooking smells because we had to eat, have food. There wasn't much in the way of washing facilities and then we had to fight a war at the same time.'

He was now back in Britain, on assignments along the coastline of occupied territory, Norway in particular, spying and running clandestine operations, the stuff about which novels are written and films made.

'I was never a dashing leader,' he says modestly, but he won the DSO (Distinguished Service Order) and the DSC (Distinguished Service Cross) for his operations, and he commanded submarines in the Mediterranean and in the Far East, where he sank a big Japanese submarine as it hunted his vessel. For this he was decorated with a second DSO.

'I must have inherited something from my predecessors in being able to survive for the entire war in submarines. No other commander did. I would hear of my friends going missing, their submarine disappearing, other young fellows would come up the line and be appointed commanders and they too would be lost. I managed to get right through the war, from start to finish. I got known as a "lucky commander" so those who sailed with me also felt lucky I suppose.'

But surely there was some particular experience, some trick, something he used that helped him more than anyone else?

'One thing I always did was to take note of the wind direction before diving below the surface. When we fired torpedoes at an enemy ship there was a strange feeling. They were our enemies, but when the torpedo hit many of them were going to die and I was the one who had made the decision that killed them. But it was war and we had to protect ourselves too.'

So, when he attacked the enemy, he would next order his submarine to dive as deep as possible and when at that depth, would motor upwind, using the directional knowledge from the surface conditions he had noted before he dived.

'Enemy warships would often tend to turn their engines off to listen for the noise of our submarine and they would drift downwind as they did this, so we were well below and always moving away from them.'

The end of the war was a blessed experience of peace, but the years in submarines had taken their toll on Bill's health. Bad food – submarines were not great places for cuisine – the stress of constant danger, the lack of oxygen in the system, were factors. Then he thought about going mountain climbing.

'I fancied Everest, but I hadn't the strength for it, a lot less after the war, but I thought of trying sailing.'

So he crewed as a navigator in the Fastnet and Bermuda yacht races. He began delivering yachts to earn money, married and bought a castle.

'Not a bad way to live, even if money was tight in those days.'

He and Anita joined in the Galway social life and rode to hounds, hunting foxes, with the Galway Blazers. So when in 1949 he could afford his own first boat, he called it *Galway Blazer*. He sailed it alone across the Atlantic from Gibraltar to Antigua in twenty-eight days, where he was joined by Anita and their first son, called Tarka Dick. 'We named him after the novel *Tarka the Otter*. It was a story I really loved.'

Anita had difficulty with sea sickness, unless she had hold of the tiller, so she helmed and Bill looked after the baby down below while they sailed.

But money was a problem and *Galway Blazer* was sold three years later, after which Bill turned to work on the land around his castle at Oranmore. It was tough to make a living. Bog and rock challenged his efforts, but they managed and he and Anita got him some sailing with friends in Brittany and Greece.

In 1968 *The Sunday Times* announced its Golden Globe solo race around the world. It was the first ever of its kind and legendary figures in the sailing world entered, including Robin Knox-Johnston, Chay Blyth and Bernard Moitessier. The notorious Donald Crowhurst entered, but he falsified his yacht logs and reported false positions by radio, giving the impression he was winning with superb sailing speed. In those days there was no GPS or satellites available to monitor the progress of the yachts.

'It also meant we were entirely alone, totally dependent on ourselves and with little chance of rescue if things went wrong.'

Crowhurst disappeared off his boat. When the yacht was found, so were all the falsified logbooks.

Bill entered and contacted his wartime friend and legendary campaigner, Blondie Hasler, who favoured the junk rig and had proved its abilities, sailing his yacht, *Jester*, single-handed. Bill raised the money for the race and for a specially-designed, forty-two-foot junk-rigged *Galway Blazer II*. The design was done by Angus Primrose and she was built by Souter's yard in Cowes, the yachting centre of the UK.

'I made my worst mistake ever at sea in her,' Bill admitted.

A thousand miles out of Cape Town in South Africa, he ran into a hurricane. *Galway Blazer II* was running before the wind, but Bill was getting tired and worried.

'I was steering,' – the benefits of self-steering for long periods were not yet developed – 'and I thought that I might get tired, so I decided to lie a-hull.'

This is the recommended method of riding out a storm when the crew feel they can no longer cope with the conditions. But *Galway Blazer II* capsized, rolled and was demasted. Bill used two alloy poles to make a jury, a temporary sailing rig system, and limped into Cape Town after many days.

'I was lucky there. I met a former submariner contact who was working for a shipping company and he got the yacht shipped home for me at no cost.'

The following year *Galway Blazer II* was repaired, refitted and re-rigged by Souter's. A new junk rig design was attempted to get the boat to sail closer to the wind. Bill was determined to try again for a solo circumnavigation of the world. He set off from Plymouth but the rig wasn't a success and he abandoned the attempt, putting into Gibraltar.

The yacht was again taken back to Cowes and the original junk rig installed, so a year later, September 1970, Bill set off again to sail around the world. This was an individual attempt, 'something I wanted and was determined to do'. There was none of the high-powered, lavish sponsorship and publicity attached to attempts these days.

He got to the toughest area of all the world's maritime regions, the Southern Ocean, when the cold polar air caused him a lot of problems.

'The skin was peeling off my hands. I didn't have the

equipment of today … I knew I would be in trouble if I kept going … My hands were going raw, I wouldn't be able to sail the boat.'

Again, he had to divert to a port for help and headed for Fremantle in Western Australia. Turtle-oil, surgeons' waterproof gloves and explorers' Antarctic-type gauntlets were acquired and he set sail again, but despite all his determination, he was to be blocked again. This time a great white shark was waiting.

'We were sailing well, seven days out from Fremantle when I heard this terrible bang on the port [left-hand] side. I looked down into the boat and could see a hole through which water was pouring. In all the time I have been at sea, seeing the water pour through that hole in the hull was a really bad time.

'I thought the only thing left to me was to ring up God and ask for help, but there was no answer, or he didn't hear me! So I had to do something myself. I tacked the boat, putting it about, switching to the other tack, so that the side of the boat with the hole in it was out of the water. Then I got lines to tie a sail with and rigged it around the outside of the hole. This was a wooden boat, so on the inside I got a piece of timber which I braced against the broken plywood in the hull and pushed them back into place. The water came in in less quantities than it had. It stopped pouring in and was only squirting, so I managed to get the boat back to Fremantle again. There a shipwright repaired the boat for just £50. A decent man who would not make a lot of money from that repair but wanted to help me.'

Bill was unfazed. With the determination that has characterised his life, he was determined to continue his efforts to circumnavigate the world. In December 1972 he left Fremantle again. The turning point for the circumnavigation would be

Cape Horn, which he rounded into 1973 and completed his round-the-world solo sail into Plymouth. Success at last, and his efforts won him the prestigious American Cruising Club Blue Water Medal.

Last year Bill King was decorated by the British Ministry of Defence with the newly created Arctic emblem for service in he Arctic regions during the Second World War.

With Anita, Bill wrote four books about his experiences – including *The Wheeling Stars* and *Capsize*. Anita also wrote a book about the famous Francis Chichester, who sailed *Gypsy Moth* around the world, and another about cruising in the Caribbean with Bill, called *Love in a Nutshell*.

8

TOLLING THE BELL
AT THE BIGGEST GRAVEYARD
ON THE IRISH COAST

The bell chimed out, its sharp metallic sound a contrast to the stillness as the Courtmacsherry lifeboat rolled in the gentle swell. Then three wreaths were tossed onto the water and began to float slowly away. Lifeboat mechanic Michael Hurley moved away from the bell he had been ringing and gazed across the sunlit water towards the Old Head of Kinsale. There was a thoughtful look in his eyes; there was emotion unspoken as he gazed across the miles of open water. His eyes were resting on the distance, imagining a different scene:

'We were out here one year with the Merchant Navy Association from Barry Dock in Wales, all strong men who had seen and experienced a lot at sea themselves and lost companions and relations during the Second World War and they all had tears in their eyes, imagining what it must have been like for those aboard the *Lusitania*.

'The sudden hitting of a torpedo, then passengers who had been at their lunch onboard, now fighting for their lives in the water out here. It's the biggest graveyard on the Irish coast.

'Imagine that where we are now, there were hundreds of

people fighting for their lives. It's a place that could be creepy. It must have been an awful sight. When the bow hit the bottom, the stern was sticking up out of the water. Imagine that and the screams and cries of the people struggling to live, while others died beside them.'

I was with the crew of the Courtmacsherry lifeboat on the ninetieth commemoration of the *Lusitania* sinking, a man-made disaster on 7 May 1915 in which 1,198 people died, caused by the bitterness of war, when a German submarine torpedoed the liner.

Whatever about the political machinations of the time, or whether there was, or what caused, a second explosion aboard the ship after the torpedo struck, and whether it was carrying armaments or not (about which controversy still continues), it was a terrible tragedy.

As I looked across the sunlit waters fifteen miles south of Courtmasherry and the Old Head, on a day when the weather was similar to that of the sinking, I shared the thoughts of a lifeboatman whose task is to save lives and began to imagine what it must have been like for those struggling in the water, shocked at the sudden change from a pleasant afternoon to death close at hand, their clothes dragging them down, little time for lifeboats to be launched or lifebelts to be donned.

The people of the Old Head remember the dead of the *Lusitania* every year when they gather at the memorial they have erected overlooking the sea.

The lifeboat from Courtmacsherry which went to the rescue of the *Lusitania* in 1915 did not have the powerful engines of the modern boat to dash quickly to the scene of tragedy. It was a rowing and sailing lifeboat and the crew took several hours to arrive.

An old lifeboatman living in Courtmacsherry, Jerry Murphy, told me what the scene was like when they got there:

'There were hundreds of people in the water, live ones mixed with the dead, shouting and screaming for help. We picked up those we could and then passed them onto bigger boats. Then we tried picking up bodies and another boat shouted at us – "Leave them, there's plenty of other live ones still out further."'

And so the rescue went on as the crew rowed back and forth, separating people still alive from the dead. A scene of horror beyond imagination.

'We rowed back exhausted in the dark from a rescue, but also a graveyard of the dead.'

Jerry Murphy died several years before Michael Hurley spoke the same words around the same spot at sea.

The words of a lifeboatman from one generation ringing through to another.

9

FROM DERRYNANE TO THE TOP OF THE WORLD

'Sailing can be like an Elastic Band'

Derrynane on the Iveragh Peninsula is a place of special beauty. Along a narrow, winding road where at times confidence in finding the harbour disappears as the road circles around Caherdaniel, past the home of Daniel O'Connell the Liberator until it suddenly opens onto the harbour. On a wild day, the waves can dance and hurl themselves against the offshore rocky protector of the harbour, while inside there is safety and, in summer, tranquillity as boats swing and bob to their moorings.

Just to the east, across the sand dunes and another stretch of rocks, is one of the most unusual graveyards in the country, nestling beneath the overhang of a promontory. This was once an abbey and is still called such by the local people who carry coffins on their shoulders across the beach when there is a funeral.

Looking across this marine panorama out over the adjoining Kenmare Bay, the young man said to me:

'This is a beautiful place. This is where home is and where it brings thoughts, emotions and thanks that it was here I first learned about the sea.'

Damien Foxall became Ireland's most successful sailor ever and was raised to the top of the international sailing profession as the country's best-known yachtsman when he won the first Barcelona Round the World Race after ninety-three days non-stop at sea. It was a race for boats of sixty feet long, sailed by just two people. It never stopped from the day it left Barcelona in November 2006 to the day he and his skipper, Jean Pierre Dick from France, brought their Open 60 yacht, *Paprec Virbac*, back to the Spanish city.

It was the culmination of fifteen years' work, the first milestone of which was when I met him in Kinsale in County Cork. There was some consternation amongst the French television and radio stations and newspapers. It was the top French single-handed yacht race and all thirty competitors used exactly the same type of boat. There had never before been a non-French entrant and this unknown young Irishman had won the leg from France to Ireland. This rookie had beaten the French in the newcomers' section.

Sailing is a huge sport in France, and sailors are likely to be surrounded by admirers and autograph hunters. There is a lot of money to be earned by the best – and France has many who have made their names on the international scene. That an Irishman should challenge that unbroken Gallic tradition and do it successfully was unheard of.

Damien was bronzed, fit-looking, but somewhat shy and quiet, it seemed to me that day on the Kinsale Yacht Club marina, but it was a turning point in his career and his life. He moved to France, learned the language, developed his sailing skills and became one of the top professionals, much in demand. He also had gained a lot of experience in multi-hulled boats. The Irishman who became as French as the French themselves.

Before all of that happened, I met him at Derrynane harbour to interview him for *Seascapes* on RTÉ Radio and also for *Nationwide* on television as well as the TV News.

Another Saturday afternoon long ago, he had sat on the patio at my home in Monkstown on the edge of Cork harbour as he was about to board the ferry to France in order to develop his sailing career. He talked to us aspirant sailors, myself and my family, two of whom became professional merchant mariners, and told us how he was setting off with the goal of becoming a top world professional sailor. There was no arrogance about him, just quiet, focused determination, and when I dropped him at the Ringaskiddy ferry terminal for the Brittany ferry he said goodbye, with the promise that he would keep in touch – and so he did.

Over the years I followed Damien Foxall's career as it progressed: a non-stop round-the-world sailing record, set with the explorer Steve Fossett, who chose him specially for the task; increasing numbers of victories achieved in all types of boats; and his name associated with the fastest catamarans and trimarans. Then – disaster – when one of them capsized he was seriously injured and had to be rescued from many miles offshore by helicopter.

For a while it seemed his career might be affected but he overcame the setback. So it was that, on a late February day when the sun shone, rain clouds threatened and the wind blew the waves in dancing formation outside of Derrynane harbour, I went back there to meet him, as he relaxed in his home place, following that great round-the-world victory, in which he made Irish sporting history.

'I grew up here in Derrynane, on and in the water, windsurfing, dinghy sailing, fishing and swimming. I learned sailing with Ossie and Helen Wilson at the Derrynane Sailing School and they have always been a great support. It's fantastic here, where the mountains drop to the sea, the woods, the natural harbour. It was a fantastic place to grow up. There are few places in the world like it and despite all the travel I do and have done for work, I still haven't found any place to compare with this, really. I was always involved with the sea, so my life has been a progression I suppose.

'You hear the sound of the sea always here, it is a constant sound and in a strange kind of way it has probably influenced me over the years. That is something that has always been with me, that has influenced me from the outset. Then I was very lucky over the years to realise the potential of the marine industry and particularly the sailing industry. There are fantastic opportunities. I am very lucky to have created something out of what I love.'

So why did he leave Ireland?

To follow his career, there was no other opportunity for Foxall but to go to the countries where sailing is a much bigger sport than in Ireland, where there are no prospects for such a career. The UK, France, the United States and New Zealand are the places where yacht racing has been developed and where there was work, such as delivering boats or crewing on them.

'That drew me away from home. I sailed the French single-handed racing circuit for three years. I had to go wherever the next race was that I could get hired for. There were great experiences, but it was all away from home; that is the reality of life.'

He was invited to join the round-the-world project by Jean

Pierre Dick and while the public attention was drawn to it as they faced the tough Southern Ocean and the area known as the 'Roaring Forties,' with winds of forty miles an hour and freezing temperatures, the race itself was the final stage of a campaign which they had worked on together for many months before the event even started.

Jean Pierre Dick had first conceived the idea about four years before, while he was still sailing and winning world races. He was raising sponsorship for it and has half-a-dozen technicians who permanently work for him on developing the various sailing projects in which he takes part. It was a huge tribute to the Kerryman that Dick had heard so much about him and sought him out to be his partner for the toughest race yet planned for a crew of just two. In February 1997 Damien went to Australia where the boat for the race had been built. They sailed it together back to Europe, so it sailed halfway around the world before the race even started.

'We spent six months getting it ready in Europe, but that distance of sailing before the start was a key to our success, because every bit of gear was tested and what would break broke before the race. It was a fantastic opportunity to be asked to join such a project with a strong team around us to plan it.

'You don't just suddenly decide to do such a race. You work hard at the planning and I got the opportunity to input my ideas for the development of the boat.'

Though the yacht may be sixty feet long, much of the capacity is taken up with storing sails, equipment, food for the non-stop voyage and gear, and the bow is kept pretty bare on ocean-racing yachts so that they are able to handle waves without too much weight to slow them down.

One development on which they worked in particular was to be able to move the weight around inside the boat so that it was always on the weather side – where the wind is coming over and which would help the yacht to balance and maintain its drive and keep its momentum as the wind rose. In yachts with more crew aboard, sailors sit on the weather side, using their weight to hold the boat down.

This is all perfectly legal. Some boats now use water ballast to be pumped from one side to the other, but for those who don't have such facilities it can mean the daunting and physically demanding task of moving sails, which on these yachts can be big and heavy, from one side of the boat to the other. I remember doing it on the eighty-three-foot *NCB Ireland* in the Whitbread round-the-world race when there was a crew of eighteen aboard. It was exhausting and the crew lost weight simply from the amount of sweating it caused.

With just two aboard, Dick and Foxall devised a system where the entire inside of the cabin, which they used for sleeping, eating, navigating and whatever other duties were needed (there was no toilet, just a bucket – that's known in sailing parlance as the 'bucket and chuck it' system), swivelled round. It was a unique system that was ahead of any other boat's design in the race.

'It's a new concept. The idea of moving weight isn't new. You can be carrying maybe a ton-and-a-half of sails, safety gear, equipment, anchors, clothes, food and so on and you have to move this stuff around the boat whether you are going downwind, or turning the boat, making a tack to port or starboard, from one side to the other, back and forth. There is a huge amount of work on every tack, which could take an hour to do and that is a time constraint. On a crewed boat you have people to do it, but with just a crew of two it is daunting, so it was a fantastic concept. The whole living area swivelled around, so you could move the whole interior of the boat and when you tacked everything was in place. It was fantastic. It improved the performance of the boat and helped us too with the effort we had to put in. Other boats had not thought through to this as we had and may have been leaving equipment and so on where it was because of the effort, while we had planned for this and it did help us, particularly in the stage of the race when we got back into the Mediterranean past Gibraltar and had to put in many, many tacks to turn the boat and use the wind to the best advantage.

Damien believes in giving his best to everything he does and realised when he agreed to crew *Paprec Virbac* with Jean Pierre Dick that this race would demand 110 per cent. And there were difficult times aboard.

'There were moments in the three months at sea – anyone who has done even twenty-four hours at sea will know it – when you are cold and miserable, when you are wet, tired and you wonder "What am I doing out here? I'm going to take up another sport." But then there were the better moments: going for twenty-four hours downwind – fantastic but hard also, but satisfying. We were gaining many miles on our opponents – ten days of it, downwind with the spinnaker [the coloured sail in front of the boat, and downwind can be the best of sailing but needs total concentration] up, but it was demanding, tough, steering continuously; one mistake, one lapse of concentration and the boat would be wiped out.'

That meant that it could get out of control, lurch to one side and cause huge damage. At the speeds they were doing they had to steer twenty-four hours a day, balance the boat, try to eat, sleep and deal with their bodily needs, fuelled by adrenalin and the realisation that they were sailing much faster than their competitors. It was hugely challenging, and could be nerve-wracking.

'That was the better part, quickly followed by getting into a high pressure ridge.'

This meant less wind and they were forced off their course since they had no engine and could only follow the wind. They had led the rest of the fleet for weeks.

'We were forced very far south, into the icebergs area and we slowed right down. We were going very slow. The other boats came right onto us, from five hundred or six hundred miles back. They got an advantage with the wind they had while we had none. They came to within ten miles of us: it was terrible, you felt that all the effort you had put in was for nothing. It was crushing. All the effort we had put in, we felt, did not pay off.

'That was the hardest part. The mental effort was huge. That was a very tough part, the mental competition to keep ourselves going and we had ninety-three days of that. The important thing was to keep pushing ourselves, telling ourselves that we could get out of this and keep ahead, even when the other boats closed up on us. But we did manage to get going again. Sailing is like a piece of elastic as a sport, it contracts, then it can widen out again.'

Professional sailing is a tough business where you are as good as your last success. 'Any competition means just that you are not guaranteed a win on the start line. If you were there then there would be no point in racing. There would be no challenge. Sailing is a sport where you must get many things right, more

The *Asgard II*, the Irish national sail training vessel, which sank in The Bay of Biscay in September 2008.

The Bantry Longboat in the National Museum of Ireland, Dublin.

Storm clouds over Clogher Head in Dingle Peninsula.

The uncovering of the Barna Bog Boat in 2002.

Mick Murphy with his father's medal for service at sea during World War II.

Dun Laoghaire Harbour.

Dunmore East Memorial.

Damian Foxall at the beach in Derrynane. Damian is one of the most experienced sailors of his generation, he is a veteran of 18 transatlantic races and 7 round-the-world events.

Earthrace docked at Lapps Quay in Cork.

Fishing vessels in Howth, Co. Dublin.

John Kearon, Brendan Treacy and Oliver Ward working on the *Asgard* project.

Fishing boats in Baltimore.

perhaps than in any other sport. There are so many parameters you must get right. You must sail the boat fast all the time. The team, the crew, no matter what the size, two or more, must be right, must work together. You must line the boat up with the weather and you must be able to adapt to all the changes that different weather patterns bring. There is no sport so testing as sailing, as demanding, where you just have to concentrate all the time on getting the boat moving to its best potential and where everything can change in a few minutes and you can be fighting to survive, not just to win a race. Even if you have a lot of luck, get going well, you are not guaranteed to win: that's what the sport is all about. Things can change in a few minutes.'

Damien has had his share of disappointments and, as he says himself, failures. He has been on yachts where the worst has happened – a broken mast, being thrown overboard, etc. In 2005 he had to be rescued by helicopter after suffering injuries in the horrendous capsize of a huge trimaran during the Transat Jacques Vabre passage race.

That didn't put him off sailing – he was more annoyed with himself:

'I was more angry about that, more frustrated than anything else. We had sailed well. We were leading the fleet in the big transatlantic race. We were two days from the finish. Two years before, we had been third and we were on for the podium finish. We were going well, then in the middle of the night, the wind suddenly changed. It gust up from twenty-five to fifty knots as a front was coming through and we were changing over helms. My partner, Armel Le Cléac'h, was coming to take the helm from me and over the vessel went all of a sudden. We were sailing conservatively at the time, which had brought us to the front of the fleet. She went over before we could do anything about it. We had all the balls lined up and something didn't go right.'

There is no hope of the crew righting such a massive boat themselves. In the dark night, in the water, with the wind gusting, Damien and his partner called to each other. Damien was injured, he couldn't move one of his arms, his neck hurt, but his lifejacket had inflated and kept him afloat. He scrabbled around to get something to hold onto, part of the upturned boat. Armel was also OK and holding on, but their situation was precarious. However, the emergency beacon had been set off by the capsize and they felt help would be on the way.

As they trod water and held onto the upturned rig, which was now being blown along by the high winds and twisting and turning in the heavy seas, it was still a precarious situation. But within hours a French maritime rescue helicopter was on the scene, a welcome sight to the two sailors, who had managed to get themselves onto the rig as they waited for help.

'It was dodgy, but you go into the mode where you have had the training and you have thought what to do and you can deal with the situation. It was one of those moments when things could have gone badly wrong.'

But as a professional sailor, the only way to make a living is to get back out sailing again and that Damien did, though the boat he sailed on in the Volvo Round-the-World Race did not do particularly well.

This race is a nine-month event on a fully-crewed boat, with several stop-over ports to break the periods at sea. But it wasn't long after he finished that Damien was planning to voyage around the world again, this time non-stop and with only one other crew, a voyage that would make him a legend both in international and Irish sailing. The Kerry flag – the gold and yellow of the Kingdom – was carried proudly by Derrynane people when Damien arrived at the finish line in Barcelona.

He married a Canadian, Suzy Anne, and they have one child, Oisin, who was three months old when his father became a sailing hero. As Suzy Anne walked the beautiful area around Derrynane, she spoke about her husband's success:

'I am happy that he is doing what he likes to do. It is not the easiest job he could have, but he is doing what he likes to do. I do get worried about him, but I try not to. If I worried all the time I could not live when he is away. I trust him and am confident in him when he is away at sea, but it can be a long time. Ninety-three days was long and it particularly felt so when he was away at Christmas. It is fantastic what he has achieved, from where he started here in Derrynane.'

Damien Foxall's success should raise Irish interest in sailing, particularly amongst young people, and underline the country's great maritime traditions.

'We are good enough now not just to be participants at international level, but to win,' he says. In October of 2008 Damian Foxall left Alicante in Spain aboard the Green Dragon, Ireland's entry in the Volvo Ocean Race Around the World. With him was another Irish sailor, Justin Slattery from Cork, with whom he had set that world speed record for Steve Fossett.

Damien's father, Roger, was the first Irishman to sail a yacht from Ireland to Russia. He sailed his boat – *Canna* – from Derrynane to St Petersburg in June 1987, before the Iron Curtain came down and when it was difficult to get permission to enter Soviet waters.

10

THE SAILING ENGINEER
OF GALWAY

My first experience of John Killeen on a boat was when we were trying to get his forty-four-foot yacht, *Mayhem*, over the start line at Wicklow in the Round Ireland Race in the late 1980s. I was aboard with an all-Galwegian crew, the only Corkman amongst them. It wasn't going particularly well, with a fitful wind that threatened to push us across before the start gun went, but we succeeded and for the next five days sailed around Ireland in weather that varied from pleasant to downright awful. At one stage it bordered on terrifying, when the wind went up to forty-four knots on the nose, that is directly ahead, and the worst possible place for the wind to be on the exposed west coast of Ireland. I considered the crew and the boat from the City of the Tribes well-named – *Mayhem* by name and nature.

Night-sailing up the west coast, we had the spinnaker up and, as the wind got up, we got the boat to ride up on a wave as it lifted from the stern, then we would rush along with huge roars of enjoyment until the wave outpaced the boat and she would slow until the next one lifted her again to repeat the process.

I remember as we rushed past a darkened fishing boat there was some opinion that we might have crossed a fishing net.

A spotlight from the trawler cut a swathe of light through the darkness. It didn't see the *Mayhem*: she was travelling fast past it. Into the night went a wish from one of our crew, who suspected that the darkened boat might have been fishing illegally, 'Hope the net was tied to your toes in the bunk, you b****'.

John had a few young lads from Galway Bay Sailing Club along, and one of them asked as we rounded Mizen Head on the south coast to turn north up the fringe of the Atlantic, what the weather would be like for the night ahead. To us older hands it was obvious that the wind was freshening and you could see the change in the water conditions. 'Don't worry about what you eat, you'll be seeing it again later.' And the young lad did in the early hours of the following morning as he 'fed the fishes' – a polite way of describing seasickness. At that stage I was helming, trying to cope with an ever-increasing head wind on the nose and sailmaker, Glendys Cullen, was wrestling a sail down to reduce our exposure as the wind meter showed it whistling past thirty and up to thirty-five knots. I prayed to God, if He loved me, to let the wind go down. I must have used up all my indulgences, because it just kept on going up and eventually we had to head out to sea to ride out the weather.

I met John Killeen and talked sailing with him many times after that night. He has a huge commitment to the sport and to popularising it, as well as a strong belief that Galway could become Ireland's sailing capital. Never mind the claims of Dún Laoghaire, Howth and Cork, Galway sailors face the toughest, most open waters and difficult weather conditions from their base at Rinville near Oranmore. 'You have to be tough to sail here,' and they are right.

I have a great picture in my mind of the sight of the lighthouse on Inisheer blinking just after midnight on a dark September night as we sailed past in my son's boat, watching white water beating against the island. We had sailed the *Contessa 32* from Liverpool and Galway was to be her home port. The size and length of Galway Bay was etched indelibly on my mind over the next few hours as we sailed towards Rinville.

John is not a Galwayman by birth: he hails from Roscommon and his first involvement with watersports was when he rowed for Marist College, Athlone. He took up sailing at University College Dublin where he qualified in civil engineering and has become one of the country's most experienced offshore sailors. It is, therefore, hardly surprising that he has a great interest in the pioneering Scottish engineer, Alexander Nimmo, who directed construction of 243 miles of road in Connemara and surveyed two-thirds of the coastline in the 1820s.

Nimmo built at least forty piers, to judge by his name being inscribed on them throughout Connemara, and Killeen thinks he probably built more bridges during his time in the west than have been built since. His belief in the Scottish engineer led to his sponsoring a history of Nimmo's work by historian Kathleen Villiers-Tuthill.

John Killeen impressed me with his deep commitment to the marine sphere, while remaining a retiring, quiet man, who does not push himself or his achievements forward. He is chief executive of Cold Chon, which makes bituminous binders for road surfacing and employs over four hundred staff around the country. A sister company makes adhesive agents and emulsions which it exports and, through its activities, is one of the largest users of Galway Port. So Killeen has strongly supported the proposals that the port should relocate from the present tidal harbour to the south-east to create a larger port with better tidal access.

What I particularly like about him is his attitude – to seek solutions rather than see problems, the view of a man who knows his sailing and likes to spend as much time on the water as he can. He doesn't have an affinity for golf. Sailing is his sport and when he talks about how a boat of his performs, his pleasure and enjoyment of the water can be sensed.

Mayhem was one of the boats he didn't name *Nimmo*, after the engineer whom he admires. With a keen interest in arts and culture, in addition to sailing, you won't hear him speak a lot about his achievements at sea, but he loves it.

Many years ago when he was in what would be regarded as the safe sinecure of a public service job as an engineer with Roscommon County Council, his home county; he left for the tougher challenge of the private sector where, through drive, energy and ability, he has succeeded.

'Isn't it good to be alive, to be able to enjoy what you do, to be able to sail,' he said to me as we talked on a summer's evening after a racing event in Galway. Leaning on the wall of the sailing club, looking out across beautiful Galway Bay, I could agree with him and take the view that there was no mayhem in John Killeen's philosophy of life, of which the marine plays a big part.

11

THE LAST OF THE GREAT RINGSEND BOAT BUILDERS – HE HAD THE SEA IN HIS BLOOD

On the south bank of the Liffey, standing on the quay wall alongside where the old gas works used to be until modernisation brought the developers smelling profits rather than the nauseous odours of gas, is one of the most amazing artefacts of Irish maritime history – the Dublin Diving Bell. I have done news and feature reports on radio and television about the fascinating story of the tough, determined men who worked with the bell, in what would now be regarded as appalling conditions, to maintain Dublin Port.

'It shortened a lot of men's lives, working under the pressure inside it, which would flatten an empty cigarette packet and if a man had a cold, especially a head cold when he got in, he would be in a bad way in a short time, because glands would burst, he would bleed. The hearing would be affected, it would get a big bang of compressed air and the ear-drums would fill up with blood and there was then only four days to get it out, either by letting it blow itself out or getting it pumped out in hospital.'

The man who told me that story was the last shipwright to dive in the Dublin Diving Bell. He was Joe Murphy, best known as the Ringsend boat builder, a man who came from a very proud maritime part of Dublin, the last fishing village before the urbanised capital spread its sometimes unfriendly grip on surrounding communities and destroyed the uniqueness of many. Not Ringsend though, for its people still maintain a defiant type of independence and their own community structures and supports with great pride and determination.

It was in the days when computers and digital equipment had not yet taken over and I was the proud possessor of what I felt made me a real radio reporter: the great old reel-to-reel Uher, on which magnetic tape spun from one reel to another. The heavy Uher had a clear plastic cover and as the tape went through the heads, speech was recorded with a clarity that the cassettes which took over could never match.

I had heard about Joe through contacts who told me, as often happens, that this was a man who had 'great stories' and just had to be recorded. I had to reach him through other 'contacts' and, after a while, the interview was arranged for Poolbeg Yacht and Boat Club, another hallowed part of Dublin's port tradition. So, on a bright, sun-dressed Saturday afternoon I arrived at the clubhouse, which then had just a long, open downstairs area with a bar at one end. It was my first visit and I have since always enjoyed going there to sample the relaxed easy-going attitude where enjoyment of sailing and boating is evident. These days the club has built a lovely new marina, with a pontoon, but it still retains that welcoming, pleasant atmosphere.

I was introduced to Joe but it was evident that the busy clubhouse was not the place to record, so we went outside to sit on some comfortable boulders in the sun. Joe was somewhat nervous and it was decided that a pint would be no harm to 'get in the mood'. In this I had to join him, because an interviewee could not be allowed drink alone. Anyway, it might make him a bit wary of the interviewer, if he was not being equally friendly. The first pint didn't settle the situation, another one would be no harm and so it went on, with me wondering when we would get started and if I would still be in a fit enough state to do the interview.

Joe must have sensed my thoughts:

'If we keep going like this I'll have no trouble with my accent. You won't know whether it's my normal one or that I sound like it after a drink or two … Are you settled enough now to ask a few questions?'

I switched on the Uher and began, then noticed I had the pause lever down … Start again.

'You sure you're alright? Will we have another?' Joe asked, taking some advantage of the pause! So there was another brought out to us, because at that stage I was wondering about a straight line to the bar, where there were several grinning faces looking out the windows at my attempts to get the recording started.

'Here you are *Seascapes*, get that down you now and sure there'll be no trouble talking to Joe. Ask him how they managed for the calls of nature in the diving bell.'

'The Galway boys gave me the plans of the hooker after a lot of problems, but it was a good move,' said Joe, completely changing the subject.

My Uher batteries were now worrying me. I hadn't switched off after forgetting to let the pause button go.

'We'd better start, Mr Murphy …' At this stage we had been sitting, talking, or was it drinking, for nearly an hour. 'We'll do no such thing if you call me that … Now, what do you want to ask?'

There are some interviews that are an extraordinary experience. This was one of them and I got to know a man I met several times thereafter, a legend in what he did, one of the largely unknown great contributors to the maritime scene, except in his own circle, but one which spread from Ringsend to encompass the west when, reaching from Dublin across the country was not a regular thing back in the 50s and 60s.

The diving bell, which is now a unique historical artefact of which many people will still be unaware, consisted of a forty-foot-long cylinder, three feet in diameter – less than a metre – with step ladders going down into it. The bottom was twenty foot square, eight feet high and the sides were of iron eight inches thick to withstand the pressure from the water. It weighed ninety tons, with a bell float to lift it. Men worked from inside it to build Ocean Pier, South Bank Quay, Alexandra Quay East as well as oil berths. They laid foundations for caissons to be sunk to build the quay walls.

'We worked under compressed air at forty feet, five men, four labourers and myself, the charge hand which I was at the time. The men dug the bottom so much and put it up on a stage inside the bell. Fifteen tons. The bell was lifted by a lifting barge, brought to one side and then down again to the river bed and we dug away until it was flat. The pressure of the air kept out the water in the twenty-foot-square area inside the iron sides.'

It was amazing work. Health and safety regulators would have a fit about it these days and it preceded the use of diving suits.

That was just one of Joe's experiences in a life dedicated to boat building and the shipwright profession, a man 'with the sea in his blood,' as Jim Cooke of the Ringsend Technical Institute put it when he described him. 'He was the last of the great Ringsend boat builders in Thorncastle Street, a man who inherited a long and proud Murphy family tradition in Ringsend.'

The Murphys were from Wexford and it was Joe's great grandfather who set up in Ringsend, where Joe Murphy was born in 1928. He built fishing boats and, as a youngster, spent his holidays with fishermen and aboard fishing boats. During the Second World War the yard was under the control of a naval compulsory order.

At the age of fourteen, his grandfather, with whom he had sailed on the gaff-rigged yacht that he owned, bought Joe his first boat, a Lough Shinny yawl, which he converted into a yacht. He did this with the help of a more experienced man, who regularly told him, when they were checking any fitting, 'it's near enough!' So Joe called his first boat *Near Enough*. At Murphy's yard schooners, fishing boats, yachts and other vessels were built and conversions of boats carried out – the famous Mermaids, Dublin Wags, the 21s, all boats which Joe knew well.

After the Second World War, Dublin Corporation conducted a campaign to get rid of the Murphy yard which he then ran. It was a story of the early days of property development. A small yard, doing a good job, was described by the local authority as not justifying the space it held by the employment it gave, and when the lease ran out, the authority moved in with a compulsory purchase order to close it down. This was not to the credit of the local authority, but demonstrated again the tendency of officialdom in Ireland to know and care little about the marine sphere.

Joe was going to go to New Zealand, but his mother became ill and he remained though, as he told me, a man disillusioned after the treatment he had received from Dublin Corporation. It was one of the saddest periods of his life. The 'iron fist' of a public authority which should have appreciated maritime heritage was shown when they served him with an order to remove boats that, like many a boatyard, were on the premises but whose owners had not claimed or accounted for them. These were placed on the river, but when no one claimed them had to be broken up on the demands of the Corporation, including a Galway hooker.

Joe was asked to become a boat-building instructor for the Vocational Education Committee in Dublin, which wanted to keep these skills alive, and in later years, he taught the skills in Killybegs. He designed and built his own boats before going to work for the Dublin Port and Docks Board and so, into the diving bell.

He built boats in his spare time, 'over 200 altogether, from six-foot punts up to fifty-foot boats'. And he sailed boats and voyaged, even bringing a fishing boat back from Sweden. But perhaps the biggest challenge he faced in his career was to build a Galway hooker. At the time, to have one of those built outside the West was almost heresy – even to get the plans of one was very hard.

'In Connemara,' Joe told me, 'the art of building hookers is handed down from father to son. They don't seem to use drawings; they just know how to do it. It was very hard to get information from them as to how to build the boat. They regarded it as a close secret. I had been going down to Connemara for more than twenty-six years. My children had gone there on holidays and I had helped to repair boats there like the gleoiteogs, but they wouldn't give me the plans, the information, so it had to be a bit of guesswork as well as what I hoped I knew.'

When word got back to the West that a Galway hooker, to be called the *Naomh Mairtín*, was being built in Dublin, it was a shock, even causing some consternation. It was built for Padraig McLoughlin, who had been a chief mechanical and electrical engineer with the Dublin Port and Docks Board and who had been aboard the fishing boat that Joe brought from Sweden.

Joe had replaced two thwarts in a gleoiteoig owned at the time by Martin Oliver, who was then holder of that revered title among traditional Galway hookermen in Galway – 'King of the Claddagh'.

'Joe came down to Galway to do the repair,' Padraig recalled. 'He jumped nimbly aboard the boat and, to the horror of Martin, ran a saw through the two thwarts, removed them and then, by some sort of magic, replaced them. Martin remarked that Joe wasn't a bad carpenter and, coming from Martin Oliver, that was praise indeed.'

Approaching retirement, Padraig wanted to build a Galway hooker and discussed the project with Joe, who considered it and, despite the problem of getting information from Connemara, produced plans.

'Work commenced, I was the apprentice, he the master and for three years it was a way of life. Finally it was finished and we sailed it around the coast to Galway.'

Joe laughed at the thought.

'They were surprised, the Galway fellas, when we built it and sailed it back to them, but it proved to be one of the fastest hookers of the lot. I enjoyed building it and fastening it with square iron, which I had to learn about because the boats were fastened like that before nuts and bolts came along and I found out the secret of doing it. Having seen photographs we got the offsets and we built it.'

But everything didn't work out easily. The offsets are the measurements of the different sets of a boat so that an identical one can be produced. But the boat they had seen and were calculating from was different and it took five sets of drawings before Joe could work out the correct ones.

'But we got it right.'

They did, however, miscalculate also on the name, because Padraig first called it the *St Martin*, which did not go down too well in places like Spiddal, so it was changed to the Irish version, as all the Galway hookers use.

The success in building that boat was to be the start of an unlikely connection between the 'inner city yacht club', as Poolbeg has been described, and the Connemara sailors. Poolbeg is credited with being one of the places where the revival of interest in the hookers was developed, Joe's work – like much else he did – being an integral part of it.

Another boat, a 'sister ship' to the *Naomh Mairtín,* was built and today it is not unusual to see a Galway hooker in the river close to the Poolbeg Club.

Joe has sailed Galway hookers in the West, to the legendary places they frequent – Kinvara, Spiddal, the Claddagh, Roundstone, Cleggan and other locations.

The importance of the Galway hookers to Irish maritime history is underlined in the restoration of boats which have been based at the Claddagh, a famous maritime part of Galway City.

I asked if he had a boat of his own.

'Not at the moment … Any boat I built for myself I always sold in a pub. I never sold one of my own boats anywhere else. It was always in a pub over a few pints – maybe I was off-guard,' he laughed as I watched the final few inches of tape edge over the recording head on my Uher. Time to switch off before the machine did it for me.

So, what was his greatest pleasure from a long career?

'I made hundreds of friends and there are people in many places, some who I trained, others for whom I built or repaired boats, who remember me as the Ringsend boat builder.'

12

MOL POL

I can't remember when I first heard *of* Moira Kearon, but I certainly remember when I first heard *from* her. She phoned *Seascapes* and told me she was in a pub overlooking a harbour on the west coast of Ireland. Furthermore, she was in front of a roaring fire enjoying alcoholic refreshment. She then proceeded to tell me that you could cruise anywhere in a twenty-three-foot boat, provided that you 'holed up' and never bothered to go sailing when the weather was bad. And the best place when it was bad seemed to be in front of a roaring fire, wrapped around a 'hot Irish'. That was the 'summer' weather in which she was sailing around Ireland.

Listeners love it when a presenter is made fun of by an interviewee. It goes down well with the public and, if the presenter or interviewer is a good professional, they will use the occasion to their advantage. When I was trained in RTÉ there were legendary broadcast professionals from whom you could learn a lot – Charles Mitchel, Maurice O'Doherty, David Timlin, Don Cockburn. We were taught in those days that the interviewee was the most important person, not the interviewer. When you were assigned to a news story you had to get the permission of the television news chief sub-editor before you could do a piece to camera, where the reporter is seen on screen.

Nowadays, regrettably in my view, egos dominate much of radio and television broadcasting and the presenter is considered more important than the participants, without whom, in speech radio in particular, and also on television, the presenter would not exist or succeed. I do not have a high regard for the concept of the presenter as the focus point or the main attraction of the programme and do not have a love of the approach of naming programmes after their presenter. To me, this is motivated by commercialism rather than programme decisions. The quality of the presenter is important, yes, but the most important focus of a good radio or television programme should be the subject, the interviewee, the story.

Moira was a case in point. On her first interview on *Seascapes*, from Arranmore Island off Donegal, if I remember correctly, I was impressed that she was from Dún Laoghaire Motor Yacht Club and was sailing around Ireland in that twenty-three footer, so I presumed that she had made remarkable progress to reach Arranmore in only a few days. It was a blowy evening outside and she was sheltering from the weather, but Moira was in good form:

'And you made it to Donegal already?' I asked in amazement.

'Do you know anything about sailing?'

Moira has always been blunt in her comments.

'Well you're from Dún Laoghaire and you only started out a few days ago and you're in Donegal now. How did you get there so quickly?'

'We put the boat in the water at Galway, we trailed it to there.'

So was the voyage of *Mol Pol* explained and, to listeners, it must have been a joyous exchange of the increasing incredulity of the presenter, matched by the calm response of the dignified lady with the hot drink in her hand in the pub. She was such a tonic, if she would excuse that description!

Moira Kearon attracted a strong listenership and we talked to her several times as she made her way northwards around the top of Ireland, then back southwards to Dún Laoghaire.

Somewhere along the way I revealed her most closely-guarded secret – her age! So in ports she called to, people began to welcome her as 'the old lady of the sea'! Her sailing companion was a family friend of many years, Owen Hearty, a former Met Eireann staffer who understood the weather and navigation, thankfully from Moira's point of view!

Moira, Owen and myself became good friends and we chronicled further voyages which they made in subsequent years. They were, to me, an example of how to enjoy sailing, a heartening change from the pomposity which can accompany some of those who talk about their boating prowess.

Moira and Owen put miles under the keel without too much stress and strain. Each season they would plan their voyage, launch *Mol Pol* at the Motor Yacht Club and sail southwards. In the DMYC in Dún Laoghaire she was regarded as one of its 'founding forces' and remained through the years as one of its driving forces. I would get a call when they reached Cork, usually berthing at their favourite haunt at East Ferry marina, where we would meet and chat and where they introduced me to their specially-made Irish coffees.

In the twenty-three-foot bilge-keeler, not a design of boat that goes particularly well to weather nor moves too fast, there is not a lot of space, but it was amazing how they had maximised every inch and the store of food and drink they carried aboard.

Invited to have an Irish coffee, the preparations would be made, the kettle boiled, the whiskey and the coffee fetched. Then when all was ready, Owen would approach with a wicked-looking, big, long injection needle. Moira had been a nurse and she revelled in this performance. As you mentally quailed and wondered what on earth was going to happen next, he would inject the needle into the coffee and the result was an excellent blending of whiskey and cream – beautiful – and a bit of a relief after that wicked-looking instrument.

Moira and her husband Stan had sailed *Mol Pol* for many a mile before he died. She was a Seamaster, Bermuda-rigged, with a twenty-nine-foot-high mast, built of fibreglass by Seamaster Limited at Essex, designed by the famous Laurence Giles. Moira told me that hers was the only Seamaster that had crossed the Irish Sea and the English Channel several times 'and cruised a lot of seas'. Her husband Stan and herself bought the yacht in 1974 and thirty years later it was still sailing. It was well known around the coast of Ireland, having sailed to Scotland, Wales, around the south coast of England and over to France into that country's canals and rivers.

Stan's death was a blow to Moira, but she is a determined lady and, with the family friend, Owen, *Mol Pol* sailed on and became a great example of how to enjoy sailing. It showed that a big boat, which seems to be the goal sought by so many people these days, with all the facilities of such vessels, is not necessary.

Certainly it was not in *Mol Pol*'s case and one of Moira's proudest achievements was taking the boat into the centre of Paris: 'For any yachting person, entering Paris by water is very special. There we were, a small boat, and there was great excitement at Port de Paris Arsenal where the marina was. They were all waiting for *le Bateau Irlandais*.'

They had some interesting experiences along the French rivers and canals. While waiting to enter Ecluse Fountaine they tied *Mol Pol* to 'quite a large tree' on the river bank. The tree began to creak and 'came straight out of the ground, partially landing on the deck of *Mol Pol*'. Fortunately, no major damage was suffered.

One problem they had was that their engine gear boxed because of *vitesse fatigue* and that made them regular visitors to a pub/restaurant at Chauny where there was a cheer every time they entered, still suffering from *vitesse fatigue*.

'All the truck drivers seemed to have their meals and beer in this establishment, which was across a bridge at the beginning of the town and, when they use a place in France, it is a good recommendation. At that time the Irish soccer team was playing in the World Cup, so when we would arrive there would be chairs placed in front of the television to see the match and there was more and more interest when Ireland kept winning. The whole pub would wait for us to arrive and the first question would be about *vitesse fatigue* and when we said *oui* there would be a big cheer and the evening would start,' Moira told me.

Eventually, two mechanics arrived from Antwerp with a reconditioned gearbox.

'We had contacted our bank at home to transfer money for the job to the bank in Chunny and as the day went on and the work was being done, I went to the bank for the money – several times! It wasn't arriving. From the bridge I would wave at Owen to indicate "no money" as the mechanics worked away. They had to be paid on the completion of the job and time was running out. I crossed the bridge several times, found a telephone box and rang the bank at home. Owen was telling the mechanics that the engine was not aligned properly with the gearbox to gain time. I think he was right probably the first time, but the second time was a delaying tactic! Finally I got sorted with the bank. The problem was in the bank in Chunny. The money had been sent all the time from home, but an official in Chunny had mislaid the fax with the information!'

She and Owen had a great approach to sailing and a love of the sea, but always with care. If they got caught out in bad weather, it wasn't for lack of planning as they would usually be heading to a harbour in advance of the onset of the intemperate period. Then they would rest in port for as long as it took, until the weather suited them again, upon which they would venture forth. 'Beyond Force 4 and we are not moving' was their rule, and so they enjoyed their sailing.

One of the greatest tributes paid to her happened on return from one of her voyages in *Mol Pol*.

'We had left Ardglass at 6.15 a.m. after staying there for eight days because the weather had been bad and that was in late August. But the weather changed for the better and so we moved on. It was calm, but very chilly. Around 1400 hours the wind changed and, with a very big tide, conditions became quite uncomfortable. *Mol Pol* coped very well but Lambay did not seem to get any nearer. However, we rounded the Bailey and it was quite nasty at this stage.

'When we got into the bay we had a short, rough sea with lots of white water. It must have been "rush hour" in Dublin Bay as every ferry and container ship seemed to appear from all angles. Our esteemed navigator, Owen, dealt smoothly with it all but then Dublin Radio [the marine, coastal and port maritime radio service] contacted us on the VHF and a few times asked for our ETA [estimated time of arrival], and I wondered why they were doing this. We were not causing any difficulties. Then, as we arrived in the outer harbour area off Dún Laoghaire, the Motor Yacht Club's launch appeared, with the club's head boatman, Tony, the club commodore and other club members, with klaxons and horns sounding. Then Captain Jim Kennedy, in full regalia, stepped off the launch and asked "permission to take over the ship" as the port pilots would do.

'He took us in to the pontoon at the club and there was a huge welcome, with banners, flowers and so on, and Captain Kennedy presented me with a Dublin Pilotage Certificate – no charge! – and said it was in recognition of the voyages of *Mol Pol* and "one for the scrapbook". It was a marvellous homecoming.'

Moira has seen eighty on her years of voyaging through life and has had to have, as she says 'part of me dealt with medically to keep going', but retains an undiminished enthusiasm for sailing and the sea. Her approach is an absolute inspiration for living life with verve, enthusiasm and enjoying it to the maximum.

13

THE FISHERMAN
FROM THE CITY

There are not too many radio reporters on the road like myself in these modern times, who travel with the recorder always ready and are prepared to stop off at the roadside to get an interview with a person they have just seen, when something tells you in your mind that you are going to get a good piece of radio. It can be a leap of faith, of trust, but generally people are kind, friendly, responsive. Journalism nowadays is a more organised activity with the formal interviews, the arranged news conferences, or the breaking news story where there is the instant reaction or the 'soundbyte' used to justify what are often the briefest interludes of actuality sound. Improvements in the quality of telephone communication has led to it being used, too often in my view, to replace the hard slog, the footwork of the reporter on the ground, meeting people who are not on the easily-reached 'contact list' – the ones who pop up regularly across all the radio stations.

My training was always to have the recorder ready and to seize the opportunity when it came. As the reel-to-reel Uher was replaced by the cassette machine which in turn was replaced by the recorder with the sound card, equipment got lighter and easier to carry, although part of me still yearns for that great feeling of using the Uher with its magnetic tape and the reels spinning around, where you saw what was happening. There is no doubt that quality has improved. The cassette had its difficulties with a tape hiss that had to be filtered out in studio, but the sound card has made recording close to studio quality when handled properly, although there are times when the length of your arm is important!

I was trying, without much success, to record the sound of water lapping the shore when I saw a man whose leisure time enjoyment made a lasting impression on me. His philosophy of life, the views of the 'ordinary man', have a strong relevance to today's Ireland and would that his views would be applied. I was on the edge of Loughaderra Lake on the main N25 road between Cork and Waterford, one of the biggest rainbow trout lakes in the country. The local Ballintotis Development Association was opening new angling facilities, a nice floating pontoon where anglers could tie up their boats instead of wading ashore, and with a car park and picnic area. I had worked there way back in the 1960s when I first started out on journalism as a reporter with the local newspaper, the *Southern Star*.

Having recorded an interview with the association's representative, I wandered off to get a bit more of a 'feel' for the story. This is what makes a 'location' report in my view. Radio is the 'theatre of the mind'. You use sound effects to bring the listener to the location. Every listener might imagine what it looks like in a different way, but with the sound effects you give them more than just a recorded conversation. Traffic whizzes past Loughaderra at a fair lick, so the noise of the lorries and cars was too noticeable on the recording, no matter what part of the lake I tried, and I was not getting that feeling of 'tranquillity' about which the association's spokesman had been rapturous in his comments.

Then I spotted him – well out in the thirty-one-acre lake, a man fishing away in a small rowing boat and thought he would make a picture for the *Seascapes* web page on the RTÉ site. People like to see what is being spoken about, if possible, so I snapped off a few photos and then he began to row towards the shore. I sat on the wall watching as he came closer but then he turned and went farther up the bank, calling to someone on shore. I stuck the camera back in the car, grabbed my Marantz, my recorder, and headed after him.

It turned out to be a fascinating chat, difficult as it was to record, because the bank was too high and steep to get down into the small boat and he could not get out. Anyway, he looked comfortable and happy in the boat and you have a better opportunity of a good interview when the interviewee is happy and contented where he is! I told him who I was and, thankfully, *Seascapes* opens many opportunities.

He was sixty-nine-year-old Patsy Quilligan from Churchfield on the north side of Cork City, a great part of Leeside. Invention is the mother of inspiration, so I grabbed one of his oars and pulled him closer to shore where the chap he had been calling to on the bank held onto it. This, it turned out, was one of his sons and so we recorded the interview with me leaning out with the microphone as far as I could, hanging onto the bank by the other hand! What a picture that would have made, only there was no one around to take it.

Paddy was an angler 'all my life … My grandfather, my father, my sons, my brothers, the whole family down through the generations.'

'So, what is the attraction of angling?' I asked him.

'Firstly you get away. You get out. It's quiet. You get to being with yourself and liking it when you get a bit of quiet time. It's peaceful: you can think and you can fish and you can enjoy being out in the air.'

It was a sunny, crisp, early spring day.

'Look, today is beautiful, isn't it? What can beat being here? You get out of the city and get a few hours of enjoyment on the lake. Fishing is cheap once you buy the rod, the reels, the licence, a little boat that you can use or even hire if you had to. You could go into a pub with €50 to €60 and it wouldn't last a couple of hours. I tell you, if the young fellows took it up today, there would be far less trouble around the place.'

His easy – and accurate – philosophy was refreshing and, for a man who spent his life in Cork City, he knew the countryside and the places to fish.

'I also fish Killarney lakes and other lakes and in two weeks' time we'll be going to Lough Conn,' he said looking at his son who was joining him on the boat for a few hours, having brought along food. Paddy had already caught a few good-sized rainbow trout, with which the lake had been stocked by the regional fisheries board.

'I always catch a fish every day I fish,' he claimed, while his son chuckled and gently challenged, 'Not always now, there are days …'

'There's no days of not enjoying the fish. You can go all over Ireland and enjoy it and meet people and it is cheap. You buy your rod, your licences and you can sit on the bank of a river or a lake all day and fish away, and there's also the wildlife to see, the birds to watch, the air to breathe. I love fishing.'

His son, more used to this particular part of the bank, more fit and energetic too, slid down and into the stern of the boat, carrying their lunch. The nice smell of fresh chips drifted back to me as they rowed out on the lake, enjoying what angling can bring, friendship born of a mutual interest.

As I put my recorder back in the car I thought of Paddy's philosophy – if young people were angling there would not be as much trouble – and of how many fathers might like to be as fortunate as he was, to share a boat and throw a fishing line in the water with his son.

14

DAMNED IF YOU DO – DAMNED IF YOU DON'T

Hugo Boyle and the pride of Achill

I went to Achill once to find out about the Sweeneys and how they might be related to the MacSweeneys from which clan I come. That search also took me to Fanad in County Donegal, where I believe some of the first of the clan set foot in Ireland when they came as gallowglass, mercenary soldiers doing the fighting for others. I also discovered that those who wrote about the Flight of the Earls in 1607 glossed over the truth to a degree which excluded the MacSweeneys from their participation in that event.

While history records the sadness this flight caused Ireland and talks in somewhat glowing terms of the earls, another record put it like this as far as the families of Donegal who had become 'more Irish than the Irish themselves' were concerned:

The earls and their families crowded aboard the vessel which on September 4 had sailed into Lough Swilly and anchored off Rathmullan ... They represented the cream of Ulster's Gaelic aristocracy, but far from being bid bon voyage by the people of

Donegal, there were angry MacSweeneys waving weapons from the shore, bitter that the Earls had seized some of their cattle as food for the journey ...

So it was that I learned that accuracy of reportage may leave a bit to be desired and that historical events may not always be recounted in totally truthful detail, nor do national leaders always do well by their people. Successive governments in this country, as we have seen, have not done the fishing industry any favours. Its troubles really began when they sold it out to gain entry to the then Common Market, now the EU.

On a wet, miserable day, with the wind from the Atlantic blowing spray and icy rain across the pier at Rossaveal in Connemara, I crossed from one boat to another at the pier. It was deepest winter, a few weeks before Christmas, and no time to be facing the Atlantic, but the man I was going to sea with was about to do just that.

A few minutes before, he had arrived on the pier carrying a briefcase, which I thought unusual for a fishing skipper – but why shouldn't he, like any man going to work? Inside it was his outline for the voyage ahead. A stocky man, he had no problem in getting from the deck of one boat to another, although negotiating a fishing boat can be a journey around lots of equipment, ropes and other fitments. I followed more gingerly, going down the side of one boat, clinging onto handholds, and up the other, before arriving on Skipper Hugo Boyle's deck.

Skipper Boyle is from Achill in County Mayo, which has a proud fishing tradition, including at one time a thriving shark fishery. There has also been a lot of tragedy in Achill. The graveyard of Kildavnet Church has monuments commemorating two of Achill's greatest tragedies – the Clew Bay Drowning of 1894 and the Kirkintolloch Fire of 1937. There is a local legend that prophesied that 'carriages of iron wheels' would carry bodies into Achill on both their first and last journeys.

When the railway arrived from Westport to Achill, on its first journey it carried the bodies of thirty-two young people from the island who had drowned in Clew Bay on the first leg of their journey to Scotland to work as potato pickers – 'tatie hoking' as it was called – because there was no other work. The boat carrying them from the island to meet a steamer to take them to Scotland overturned in Clew Bay. The railway line was closed down in the 1930s, but was used one last time to carry the bodies of ten young Achill people who had perished in a fire in a barn, known as a 'bothy,' while working as potato pickers in Scotland.

Until the end of the nineteenth century, Achill Island remained separated from the mainland by Achill Sound, even though the channel separating the two is quite narrow. High levels of seasonal migration and the importance of developing market towns emphasised the necessity for a permanent link across the narrow channel. Finance for a bridge was acquired through subscriptions collected by an interdenominational committee. A swing bridge, pivoting on one central pier, was officially opened by Michael Davitt, founder of the Land League, in 1887 and named after him. It served for sixty years, but then changes in modes of transport necessitated a wider roadway. In 1947, the old bridge was abandoned and, the following year, a new bridge opened, again called the Michael Davitt Bridge, built alongside and south of the original one.

The new bridge was the largest bridge structure to be undertaken by an Irish construction company at the time, with

J.C. McLoughlin of Pearse Street, Dublin, carrying out the work.

Cruinniú Bádóirí Acla, the Achill Yawl Festival, runs from July until September every year, with races staged at least once a week, and more frequently at holiday weekends. The yawls, traditional wooden sailing boats, which sail in the waters around Achill Island and the Currane Peninsula, are crewed by local teams, a direct link to Achill's maritime heritage. One of the best nights I spent on the water was around Achill, sailing with these yawls. The night I broadcast *Seascapes* from Achill Sound, they presented me with a three-foot model of one of the yawls, a treasure I still have with the fondest of memories.

In recent years there has been a surge of interest in the traditional Achill yawl. A new workshop has been established in Mulranny, where the traditional boat-building skills are being passed onto a new generation. The first boat to be produced in this workshop was delivered to a customer in Boston, USA, in 2003. There are also hopes to establish a permanent Yawl Centre at Achill Sound. The Yawl Festival is intended to help preserve local culture and in particular the use of the Irish language.

Hugo Boyle was very proud of where he came from, proud of his craft as a fisherman, proud of what he had achieved, and of owning his own boat. But I was in Rossaveal to meet him because he was going to leave the fishing industry, pushed out of it by increasingly rigorous and restrictive EU rules and by the neglect of the Irish government.

I have a deep respect for fishermen and I am in awe of how they can work in the most frightful of conditions at sea. I have been on heaving boats in bad weather, where my churning stomach and head have been opponents of my own body – of

Incoming tide at Youghal, Co. Cork.

Tom MacSweeney helming the *Green Dragon* in the Solent.

The *Mol-Pol* and some of her crew.

A boat tied up on the edge of Galway Bay.

Hugo Boyle's boat, the *Dé Linn*.

Howth Lighthouse.

Michael Hurley on the Courtmacsherry Lifeboat.

The Lacken Disaster Memorial.

Patsy Quilligan with a catch at Loughaderra.

Two of Clarinbridge's oystermen harvesting an oyster bag.

Calm waters in Howth, Co. Dublin.

The scenic bay of Roberts Cove in South West Cork.

Boats in Galway Bay.

my very being – as I have struggled to cope. Yet fishermen catch fish, eat, sleep and rest in these type of conditions while, below decks, they sort and grade fish. It is very tough work and they get precious little thanks from an ungrateful government, which has bent the knee so many times to Brussels bureaucrats that it is a wonder it can stand upright.

Irish waters are the richest in Europe. They should be supporting a thriving fishing industry, but because of political ineptitude, Irish fisherman are allowed to catch only a fraction of the fish in Irish territorial waters. It is a disgrace which has soured relations between fishermen and politicians and has destroyed the future of coastal communities. Ireland has no thriving fishing industry because politicians fail to understand that leading an island nation demands that the marine sphere be a priority.

'The industry has been good to me,' Hugo told me on the bridge of his trawler, *De Linn*. 'I have reared a family from it and I hope that there will be a future for the young fellows coming up, but I am not sure and I have had enough. We are over-regulated. I have no objection to regulations, they are necessary, but fishermen are badly treated.

'The department of the marine and the minister have treated us in a way the peasants were stamped on by the gentry in penal times.'

Strong language, I said to him, and suggested that there were surely also good people in the department who were committed to the future of the fishing industry.

'There used to be a time when you would get some help and advice, some goodwill, but all that is gone.'

Hugo frankly admitted that he had had his 'run-ins' with the authorities. He told me that at one stage he had been ordered not to enter Killybegs by a fisheries official, despite bad weather at sea from which he was seeking refuge, when any boat should be entitled to enter harbour for safety.

'There was no understanding shown. I came in anyway. I had given notification and I was entitled to enter. No one has the right to tell you to stay at sea when it is safer – and the correct procedure – to come in. How would farmers like to be told that they would only be allowed sell cattle at a few designated marts and would have to travel long distances to do that? That's what has been done to fishermen, who are only allowed land into certain ports and might often have to steam long distances to reach them. Farmers would not take it from the government, but that is the way fishermen are treated.'

Hugo had been prosecuted before the courts for breaches of the fisheries regulations. Like many other fishermen he deeply resented the description given in the Dáil by the then minister for fisheries, Noel Dempsey, that fishermen were 'criminals'. The Dáil had passed the Criminal Justice Bill, which included fishing offences and which fishermen claimed 'criminalised' them. There was huge, angry reaction throughout the fishing ports and demonstrations were held. There is, to this day, bitterness over the issue. Conviction gives fishermen a criminal record, just like drug-runners, thieves and so on, and it can be counted against them if they try to enter certain countries.

Mr Dempsey qualified his remarks by saying that he was only referring to some fishermen who had broken the law, but like many others, Hugo Boyle felt he had been labelled in the public mind.

'Fishing is tough enough without this attitude. Other countries do not criminalise fishermen in this way. They use administrative sanctions, a system which still applies, penalties and fines, but not a criminal record. You can get a criminal record for a small mistake in logs.'

The difficulties for fishermen at sea in tough weather in estimating accurately what fish they have of what species and so on, does not seem to register in the minds of bureaucrats in comfortable offices who issue their regulations. No one, fishermen included because stocks are their livelihoods, wants to see the destruction of stocks, but neither do they want their way of life destroyed, though gradually that is happening.

After a few hours with Hugo Boyle, I felt disturbed, sad and upset for fishermen and angry at the political neglect. This is compounded by a media where journalists just do not under-stand the fishing industry and where too many media editors ignore it until there is a disaster. Then they shed what seem like crocodile tears about the pressures fishermen are under, although they also don't even seem to know when fishermen are at sea.

Yet, despite his decision to leave the industry, Hugo Boyle, like most fishermen I have met, likes the sea and loves fishing.

'I love it, but it has changed. I can see no future for a person of my age. Hopefully there will be a future for the young lads who have bought boats and put their future in fishing.

'The government owes it to them and to the coastal regions, to ensure that there is a fishing industry in the future.'

Leaving a cold, wet, wintry Rossaveal as the night darkened the harbour and Hugo and his crew began to get their boat ready to head out to sea to make a catch and earn money for Christmas, I wondered …

15

FROM THE PHOENICIANS VIA ARKLOW TO IRISH HISTORY

I agree strongly with the motto of Arklow – as Gaeilge it reads *Maoin na Mara ar Muighin* which translates into 'In the Wealth of the Sea lies our Hope'. And it was with a man from that town that I stood when I felt a sense of history as I put my hand on the hull of what I regard as Ireland's most historic vessel, which it is his job to preserve for future generations.

Among the maritime achievements which the County Wicklow coastal town claims are that it had the first lifeboat station in Ireland, set up in 1824; that fishermen from the area taught Aran islanders how to catch mackerel; that it had the first navigation school established by the state; and is the home town of the legendary boat builder, John Tyrrell, who built the first motor fishing boat in Ireland and whose yard also built the national sail training vessel, *Asgard II*.

Arklow tradition claims that the second-century Greek cartographer, Ptolemy, charted the coastal area around the town and recorded the estuary as *Menapia*. But Arklow claims that in the centuries before Christ, Phoenician explorers landed on Clegga Strand on the south side of the estuary, into which the Avoca River flows.

It is also the home town of John Kearon and the best shipwrights in the country. So I was told when I met them engaged on what is Ireland's biggest and most important maritime restoration project – the original *Asgard*, the vessel that has its place in Irish history and which is being lovingly and carefully restored by the National Museum.

The town had a fleet of sailing ships which traded in Newfoundland, the Baltic, the Black Sea and North Africa. Its fishermen ranged the Irish coast and as far north as the Shetland Islands and the North Sea. The schooners are a proud memory in the town where nowadays yachts are moored close to the town bridge. Shipbuilding has unfortunately declined from its heyday, but the name of Arklow is still carried on the largest shipping fleet owned in Ireland.

I have other memories of Arklow.

I was once public affairs manager of NET – Nitrigin Eireann Teoranta – the state fertiliser factory, a company now closed and consigned to the realm of history. It had a big plant outside the town, close to the river, in flat land, beside the railway, a good location – but while it was a big employer, giving hundreds of jobs to the area, it was also a rather nasty polluter. The area around the plant showed it. One morning at the company's administrative headquarters in Dublin, I was told that *National Geographic Magazine* had a photograph of Arklow across two pages, showing the factory as a train passed in the early morning mist. Only, it wasn't mist – it was pollution from the factory and the *National Geographic* hadn't missed that. The photo caption told the unpleasant story!

Unusually for a fertiliser factory, NET had a maritime connection and that was some solace to me. It owned a dredger!

This was necessary to keep the harbour approaches clear for the vessels which NET used for its product. It was reckoned to be the only fertiliser factory in the world which also had a maritime corps! When that dredger was bought, it was men from the factory with seagoing experience in their former lives who sailed it across the sea to Arklow harbour.

It was at Liverpool Maritime Museum that I first met one of the town's sons, John Kearon. He was head of restoration on Merseyside and was restoring the Bantry Longboat, a boarding vessel from the ill-fated French invasion attempt of Ireland in 1796 which had landed from Wolfe Tone's ship but, in the gales which frustrated the invasion force, could not get back to the ship. It survived all those years, neglected until it was restored at Liverpool where they specialised in that work and then brought back to Ireland where it is on display in the National Museum in Collins Barracks, Dublin.

The fame and sea-keeping qualities of the Bantry Longboat have led to its being adopted in several countries, as it can be rowed and sailed. The Atlantic Challenge is an international competition which brings young people from many countries together using these boats and has spread from the West Cork bay.

I sailed on the boat that is kept in Bantry. What a great experience. There is a crew of eighteen and, without a sailing boat keel, it is balanced and held upright under sail by the weight and positioning of the crew.

John Kearon is proud of his Arklow birthplace and the history of the town. At Liverpool he also had under his stewardship the *De Wadden*, an auxiliary-engined schooner of the old Arklow fleet.

'In the days of sail, there used to be a forest of masts in Arklow,' John told me. Photographs of the period held in the town's Maritime Museum show this.

'The people of Arklow were bred and trained to get a living from the sea; they looked seaward for jobs. They were people of the sea, a great tradition.'

I felt a sense of history when I put my hand on the hull of the boat which John is now in charge of restoring, a job that will take two or three more years to complete.

Asgard, the name meaning 'ship of the gods', has not been seen by the Irish public for a long time. It used to be housed in the open, under a corrugated roof in Kilmainham Gaol, alongside the execution yard where the leaders of the Easter Rising in 1916 were shot. I stood in that yard some years ago, with a feeling of mixed emotions the day when *Asgard* was lifted over the walls and moved away for restoration by a voluntary group. I thought of the awfulness of lives ending suddenly in the rattle of rifle bolts, the wait for the thud of bullets into a body, and wondered what happened then. I thought of men who had given their lives in that yard for Ireland and of what the nation has become.

As *Asgard* was lifted over the walls of the jail, I thought of the spirit free, moving away from the trapped, imprisoned, dead body and how there was now the spirit of the vessel, which had been so much a part of the Irish freedom movement, now moving away, hopefully to a new future.

But there was no such future for *Asgard*. It was handed over to a voluntary group by the then Minister for Defence, Michael Smith. The group failed to raise the money necessary for the restoration after years of controversy over the proposal to refurbish the vessel and put it back sailing.

It was a story which I reported several times, both on *Seascapes* and radio and television news, and it became a hot topic in the media generally. Opponents said that most of the vessel would be lost, historic parts removed and it would not be the *Asgard* of history. The proponents rejected all of that and said that the place for a boat was on the water. Eventually the government intervened and took the vessel back into its ownership. Then the task was to restore it for exhibition and the best man to do that was John Kearon from Arklow, where she was built.

So it was that I stood in the old gymnasium of Collins Barracks in Dublin with John Kearon. A wall of the gym had been knocked down to get the boat in and there were two of Arklow's shipwrights with him – Brendan Tracey and Oliver Ward – men who know wooden boats and are amongst the last of the great shipwrights, a skill that, unfortunately, is dying away in Ireland.

To be Irish it is important, I believe, to understand our history and respect those who created it for us. The *Asgard* is a vessel redolent with history and it is marvellous that it is being restored under the control of the National Museum. It was at the centre of that famous episode, the Howth gun-running in July 1914, which armed the Irish Volunteers. The weapons were later used in the Easter Rising, at the birth of our national independence.

The story of *Asgard* is adventurous and brave. Erskine Childers, the father of a later president of Ireland and author of that classic espionage story, *The Riddle of the Sands*, had it built as a wedding gift when he married Molly. It was designed and built by the great Colin Archer, a legendary figure who was a marine architect and master shipwright in Larvik, Norway. They took the boat past British patrols, smuggling the guns and ammunition.

There is sadness, irony, suffering, in the story of *Asgard*. Childers was later executed by his former comrades in the terrible civil war between republicans and the Free State government.

Asgard was later sold out of Ireland, but bought back by the government in 1961 when a journalist, Liam MacGabhann, discovered her on the banks of the River Truro in Cornwall. Through his writings and lobbying, supported by friends, he brought pressure for the vessel to be acquired for the nation. Lt Joe Deasy, later flag officer commanding the naval service and now retired, sailed the *Asgard* back to Howth, the historic location of her 1914 voyage. With him were Tom Cronin, a noted Howth sailor who held a commission in the Slua Muiri, the naval reserve, and a combined crew from the naval service and the Slua.

That was on 26 July 1961 – forty-seven years to the day from when she had arrived with the guns for the Volunteers. Having been brought back, she became the navy's first sail training vessel, but records show that there were elements in the upper echelons of the naval service who did not want her and put forward various reasons why, with limited resources to keep the service itself going, they could not deal with *Asgard* as well. So, she was laid up in the Coal Harbour at Dún Laoghaire until the late Charles Haughey, a yachtsman himself, along with others got *Asgard* established as the country's first national sail training vessel in 1969.

The legendary Captain Eric Healy was her master for many years, and many other well-known Irish maritime figures were associated with Coiste an *Asgard*, set up to run the project. By the mid-70s *Asgard*, was considered to be no longer suitable for sailing and was withdrawn from training. There were some interim replacements before the new *Asgard II* was designed by Jack Tyrrell and built at the Tyrrell yard in Arklow.

Seascapes was given exclusive access to see the restoration work underway and I was honoured by the decision and delighted to meet John Kearon again. At the old gym in Collins Barracks, no longer used for military purposes, *Asgard* is only a short distance from the Bantry Longboat, of which John Kearon led the restoration in Liverpool. Life has curious ways.

So much of maritime history is dependent upon the marine sector. The work of his team of shipwrights – Brendan and Oliver and a younger man with a lot of overseas ship work experience, Paul Farrell, who hails from Galway – is meticulous. Every piece of the boat has to be checked, recorded, the details logged, and placed carefully for exact replacement as the work proceeds. There is a pride in doing it and, watching it get underway, I was proud too that this historic vessel was being restored.

Inside the hull with Brendan and Oliver, I watched as they unscrewed original keep bolts, marvelling at the construction work. Paul Campbell was working on wood pieces: 'We are learning a lot about how she was built, put together by shipwrights who did not have the modern tools of today and how well they did it … You can only marvel at their work.' The lesson of history is to learn from our predecessors and so, restoration of *Asgard* and the record of Arklow is important.

Asgard II, which replaced the first *Asgard* as the national sail training vessel, sank in the Bay of Biscay on September 11, 2008. No one was injured in an exemplary evacuation of the crew when the vessel had to be abandoned. All aboard were picked up safely by French rescue services.

16

SHOT FOR FISHING SALMON ON THE RIVER LEE AND SHAMEFUL GOVERNMENT TREATMENT OF IRISH SEAFARERS

My family tradition in seafaring goes back to 1911 when my grandfather was shot for salmon fishing on the River Lee.

Those words shocked me as Mick Murphy recalled his family's history.

'Shot for salmon fishing?' I asked with some incredulity.

'They were different times. We were under the British flag. It was their way of justice. The Ascendancy lived by different rules. He was trying to feed his family. He had a licence for draft nets, but he was doing a bit of drift-netting that night and he had no licence for that, so he was shot, just to stop him. There was a lot of shooting in those days.'

It happened down around Passage West on the river towards lower Cork harbour and Mick Murphy, in his home in Bishopstown, recounted a story in which he was adamant that his grandfather paid a strong penalty for salmon fishing without a licence.

The experience didn't stop the seafaring experience of the Murphy family. Mick's father, who had already experienced the

First World War at sea, joined the State Shipping Company, Irish Shipping when it was set up in 1941 in perilous days, when we needed seafarers to provide the food and supplies required by this island nation, which was almost completely cut off by the warring nations. Mick followed his father into the company.

He had a pride in his father, who was honoured for his service at sea in not one, but two wars.

'We said prayers at home every night for the seafarer. I remember that well. My mother would insist on it, to pray for Dad, wherever he was and in whatever conditions he was experiencing at sea.

'It never put me off going into Irish Shipping. It was a great company, but the government shut it down and betrayed the seafarers. But if it was still there I would have encouraged my sons to join it.'

Irish Shipping was the first state company ever to be put into liquidation by government decision and the seafarers were treated badly. Some were left without pensions for the war years they had served at sea in the national interest. There is still a lot of bitterness amongst former Irish Shipping employees over the way the government dealt with the company in the 1980s.

'There were great seamen in the company, but my God they were soon forgotten when the government closed it down.'

Mick went to sea first at seventeen.

'Young,' I said.

'You would be tough if you were fishing around Passage and the Cork harbour area.'

Mick was aboard the *Irish Sycamore*, a bulk carrier of Irish Shipping, at the dockside in New Orleans on 23 July 1965. She was there with a cargo of steel products and lubrication carried from the Far East, moored at the Public Commodity Wharf on Napoleon Avenue. Her master was Captain Padraig O'Shea and Mick smelled smoke and saw it drifting into his cabin.

Fire aboard ship is one of the worst things that can happen. Mick was an AB, an able seaman, and he knew immediately that there was trouble.

'Fire is deadly and particularly in the confines of a ship.'

He dashed out of his room and set off the alarm, began arousing shipmates and trying to get everybody to safety. It was seven in the morning and the fire was discovered in the crew accommodation area.

'We did our best to control it, but smoke and fire is tough to deal with. Four of my shipmates died and it was an awful tragedy and a terrible thing to happen.'

Mick was credited with being the man who saved many lives by his prompt action.

'But everyone wasn't saved. You live your life aboard ship with shipmates: you serve with them; they are part of your life. We were great friends in Irish Shipping and the *Sycamore*. I have never forgotten those who died. I never forget them; even now talking to you I think of them and I feel sorrow.'

The men who died were forty-four-year-old Patrick Cowhey, a member of the engine room staff whose wife and four children lived at Gardiner's Hill in Cork; twenty-six-year-old Thomas Ring, an ordinary seaman, from Youghal in County Cork; twenty-one-year-old Michael Walsh, a deck hand from Garryowen in Limerick; and twenty-seven-year-old able seaman William Gaule, who came from Liverpool. They had sailed with the ship when she left Cork Dockyard in March of that year. The *Sycamore* was on a time charter, operating between Far Eastern ports and the United States. The *Sycamore* continued her assignments after the fire and many of the crew did not leave the ship until she called to Gibraltar, when they were paid off and flown home to Ireland. It was nearly a year after they had left Cork port at the start of the voyage.

'I love the sea, I still do, even though I'm retired from it now,' Mick told me at the interview which we did in his home in Bishopstown, Cork. He was one of the men who formed a great corps, with huge camaraderie amongst them, who sailed with Irish Shipping.

The state company was put into liquidation by the Irish government after it ran into financial trouble, largely caused by the management of the company from onshore and poor chartering arrangements. 'It was not the fault of the men who sailed the ships, they were very badly treated.'

Seafarers took to the streets when the then Fine Gael government, led by Garrett Fitzgerald, made a decision that shut the company, stranding seafarers in various ports. It left a bitter resentment that is still evident whenever I talk to former seafarers who served with the company.

It was the first time a state company was put into liquidation and contrasted sharply with the decision to rescue Allied Irish Banks from financial trouble shortly afterwards.

On the night of 15 December 1983, the chairman of the company, William O'Neill, together with the general manager, Niall McGovern, were called to Leinster House to meet the then Minister for Finance, Alan Dukes, and the Minister for Communications, Jim Mitchell, who were accompanied by senior officials from their departments. Alan Dukes told the Irish Shipping company representatives that the government had decided that no further money would be put into the company and ordered them not to sell off any assets or create any charges to the assets. Chairman O'Neill said that this was tantamount to putting the company into liquidation, but the minister would make no further comment and told him that he would not add anything to the decision. Mr O'Neill then said that the government was walking away from the company, including the unsecured creditors many of whom were the company's employees.

The company went downhill after that and, almost a year later, on 14 November 1984, a provisional liquidator was appointed. Staff learned that from the media, before they were told by the company's board. Within minutes of the meeting, personnel from the liquidator took possession of the company and its assets. The staff of Irish Shipping felt that they were treated with no dignity.

They lost up to seventy-five per cent of their pension entitlements. There were protests on the streets before the government made compensatory gestures, and *ex gratia* payments were granted to pensioners who had risked their lives serving with Irish Shipping during the Second World War, when several of the vessels were sunk and seafarers lost their lives.

'Those men supplied the nation with its urgent needs, but they were shamefully treated. The politicians who did that should be ashamed of themselves,' said Mick. A Fianna Fáil government took office in March 1987. That party had been loud in its criticism of the way the Fine Gaelers had treated seafarers, but Fianna Fáil did nothing better, continuing to find excuses not to resolve the problem, and in 1989 the former Irish Shipping employees took legal action against the state. It is a shameful example of government neglect of seafarers that some day needs to be told in a book devoted to this appalling example of lack of political interest in the maritime sphere.

It was not until July 1994, nearly ten years after being made redundant, that employees of the company received a modest compensation package. A Fianna Fáil government approved three years' salary per year of service, which was half of the compensation proposed in 1986. Adding insult to injury, the government deducted the top rate of income tax and social welfare contributions from the compensation, even though many of the employees badly needed the money after being unemployed for several years.

'We are an island nation, but look at what the nation has done to the seafarer over the years, they have been ignored, neglected and badly treated,' said Mick. 'But I still love the sea …'

Former Irish Shipping employees still gather every year for a 'Voyage of Memories' by ferry to France and for a Christmas social.

17

JEANIE JOHNSTON

There have been times in my work as marine correspondent when I have felt a deep disgust towards people who have maligned others and sought to destroy a maritime project. Professionally, a journalist should maintain detachment from a story and be independent. When I chose the role of marine correspondent I did so with a belief that it would also be my task to inform and develop awareness of the maritime aspect of Irish life. So it has been my approach that, while reporting even-handedly to the best of my ability, I have also sought to take a positive view of developments affecting the nation.

One such was the building of the *Jeanie Johnston*, a replica of the original ship of this name, which took Irish emigrants to Canada. When I first met the man who conceived the idea, it took me on a course which led to accusations of bias, poor reportage, and disagreement with politicians, media colleagues and superiors in RTÉ. I reported on a project that I believed would benefit Ireland and raise awareness of the country abroad and of our maritime history and the story of our emigrants.

For many readers, their knowledge of the *Jeanie Johnston* will be coloured by media reporting of the time. There were journalists, both in Kerry and nationally, and similarly politicians, who never passed up an opportunity to 'have a go' at the *Jeanie Johnston*. Frankly, that irked me, for they showed little or no conception of the ultimate value of the project. I determined, quite rightly in my view, to attempt balance within the confines of correct, professional news reporting, but also to express qualified comment in the more relaxed, informative way allowed on *Seascapes*.

The project was conceived by John Griffin, a member of the staff of Tralee Urban Council and a man whom I had grown to respect for his dedication to the ideal of public service in a practical way, but who wound up as the 'whipping boy' of others. John Griffin had amazed me some time before, when he put forward his idea of reconstructing the eighteenth-century Blennerville Windmill, then a stump standing on the edge of Tralee Bay, where urban Tralee met maritime, along the old ship canal. I remember even now the office in the council building where John worked, as he unrolled his plans to do an interview with me for television news, proclaiming to the unconvinced camera crew and myself that the windmill would work again, its sails would turn, it would grind corn and be a big tourist attraction for Tralee.

I left that interview thinking that this would never happen. I was wrong. It stands today doing all of the things John said it would, a proven, valuable tourist asset for Tralee and, in my opinion, a testimony to him. However, John is gone from his job and his reputation, his career, took a battering from the criticism of the *Jeanie Johnston* project.

When John told me about his idea to build a replica of the sailing ship which had taken Kerry emigrants to Canada I had some doubts that it would become reality, but less so than I had

had about his idea for Blennerville. After all, that had worked. Unfortunately, building a ship is a different task, particularly a wooden one. The project, which started off with an estimated cost of about IR£5m and plans for a 2000 Millennium voyage to North America to recreate the original emigrant journey, got bogged down. Costs escalated and there were times when it seemed the project would be abandoned. Of course, as always, there were those who jumped on the bandwagon seeking advantage for themselves. There were many of those in political, business and media circles in Kerry and nationally. Fortunately, there were also those prepared to stand up and be counted, believing in the ultimate goal.

The decision to rebuild the famous nineteenth-century ship was taken to remember and honour the courage and will to succeed of the pioneering Irish Famine emigrants. The promoters of the *Jeanie Johnston* project also opted to retrace the voyage of its famous predecessor. A special company, the *Jeanie Johnston* Memorial Committee, was set up in 1994. The intention was that the *Jeanie Johnston* would be part of the shared heritage of Ireland, the United States and Canada.

At Blennerville, in the shadow of the windmill, was the port which was home to the original ship. There the project promoters built a special shipyard, which incorporated workshops to house the shipbuilding equipment, a protective shelter and visitor viewing gallery, offices and exhibition rooms. A group of three hundred experienced craftspeople and apprentices from the United States, Canada, Australia, England, New Zealand, Denmark, Sweden, Scotland and Ireland were recruited. But, most importantly, there were to be young people from Northern Ireland and the Republic from across the 'religious divide', who would work alongside each other in an extraordinary effort at a difficult time in Ireland to develop understanding of each others' culture. In a few words, one of those young people would later teach me a lesson that I would remember, many thousands of miles from Tralee.

That there were failures is undoubted. It was conceived as a joint project between Tralee Urban Council, Kerry County Council and Shannon Development, but the escalating costs could not be contained and the government was called on for help, which John O'Donoghue, the then Kerry minister, helped obtain. The vessel was the subject of Dáil debates as dates for the American voyage were given, then deferred, and goodwill was lost and problems mounted.

There were good people who gave of themselves, their time and their reputations to keep the project going when it seemed that it would fail. I remember people like David Irvine of the PUP in Northern Ireland who, at a very troubled and dangerous political time, committed himself to the project. He travelled to Tralee to support it and told me many a time that it would help in creating mutual understanding north and south. He deserves great credit for his commitment. There were others, such as Jim Finucane, a businessman in Tralee, who gave much of his personal and family time to keep the project alive, and Dr Henry Lyons, people who in the most difficult times were always ready with a word of explanation or to keep in touch with me. This is not to exclude others not mentioned here. There were those who built the ship and sailed on it, people like Peter O'Regan who believed a tall ship was a living thing – members of the crew later told me they believed that in the roughest times at sea the ship talked to him.

I admit to having a strong feeling of support for the project and was repulsed by those who sought to destroy it, passing off their views as concern for public monies. There were local and national politicians and local authority officials whom I still view as hypocrites. They criticised the project but were seen on the quayside at Fenit when the *Jeanie* returned from her successful voyage to North America, pushing themselves in front of the television cameras in their anxiety to be associated with what was now a success. Those kind of people I despise.

The project went well over budget. The original conception was in the region of IR£5m and it was pushing double that. Cost control was a problem and the project could have done with more involvement of maritime and ship management experts at an earlier stage, but to concentrate on those shortcomings and to ignore the overall concept was to me, quite wrong. So I began to be the voice which took a more balanced view in my reportage, telling the story of the shortcomings certainly, but also keeping in mind the ultimate aim.

This is not an attempt to chronicle the entire *Jeanie Johnston* story, which hopefully some day will be told in full. My purpose here is to record how those who should be leaders failed again where the marine sphere is concerned.

The ship eventually made its voyage to North America in 2003. One of the most emotional calls was to Grosse Isle, an island in the St Lawrence River, where it had originally docked with Irish emigrants aboard. From there it went on to Newfoundland and in its main port, St John's, I saw Newfoundlanders on a bad, wet, miserable day with a gale blowing, queuing to go on board. These were people who were generations removed from Ireland, whose forebears had emigrated and who had never been properly acknowledged by the Irish government. They touched the wood of the ship; they talked to the crew. There were tears of emotion. For them this was the recreation of what they had been told about, of Irish people arriving on a sailing ship after voyaging across the Atlantic. I thought that day of all those politicians and the media in Ireland who had sought to destroy the concept of the ship, who had criticised and found fault at every turn and I felt a deep disgust about them.

In the saloon of the vessel I talked to teenagers from Northern Ireland and the Republic who had sailed together as part of the young people's project. I was taught a lesson by a girl from Dublin. With my rather more elderly, perhaps prudish approach, I looked at her, a teenager with a ring in the side of her nose and was not impressed. I admit, these decorations were not part of my upbringing, but I should not have allowed appearance to influence me. We all make mistakes!

'And how did you get on together?' I asked. 'Did being from the north and south and from different religions divide you?'

'Mister,' she replied and I detected a somewhat withering gaze, 'there is no "I" in team, nor in crew and that's what we were and are.'

To which there was loud cheering and applause from the rest of the young people. I gleaned that there were no individuals amongst a ship's crew and they had all united together. I should have known better: she taught me a lesson.

I would wish the *Jeanie Johnston* taught Irish politicians a lesson about the maritime sphere. But even when it returned in success, commanded by Captain Tom McCarthy, with my son, Rowan as second officer, after a tough and challenging voyage in winter from Newfoundland across the Atlantic, its future remained uncertain.

It is hard to credit that even after 100,000 visitors had gone aboard the ship in North America, our government could still not see its importance and came near to selling it out of Irish ownership. To the credit of Kerry Co-op, they stepped in to save her and later the Dublin Docklands Authority bought her.

As I said, some of the journalists writing about the *Jeanie Johnston* disgusted me and the comments made by various politicians were appalling. One which I remember was made in the Kerry County Council chamber by a councillor who said that the ship should be 'burnt in Brandon Bay'.

I also took umbrage at the senior RTÉ executive who took issue with me because he felt I was giving too much coverage to the story and told me that the best thing which could happen to the ship would be that it would be 'wrecked on some shore'. At the time my son was an officer aboard and I reminded this man that life was precious and that seafarers were as entitled to their lives as everyone else and that, if he had any pride in being Irish, he would have pride in what this ship achieved. Like many others he was blind to the sea, ignoring our maritime heritage. Too many still do, which is why the story of the *Jeanie Johnston* saddens me in one way, but in another evokes pride for those who stuck with an idea and saw it through, despite the opposition of those of less standing.

The *Jeanie Johnston* returned from Newfoundland after a tough voyage and surviving a Force 11 en route, proving the ability and work of the Kerry shipbuilders one of whom, Peter O'Regan who was the engineer, came from a family with a long tradition of boat-building. His home at Ventry is a trove of models of boats which he has built. Today he is manager of Dingle marina. The *Jeanie* was bought by the Dublin Docklands Authority, to their credit, and sails on, under charter to Rivercruise Ireland, an operator based in West Cork.

18

ROSSLARE'S PROUD LIFEBOAT TRADITION

I was once held captive inside a barricade at Rosslare harbour and abused by fishermen and their families from Kilmore Quay. Rosslare is the base for ferry operations to the UK and France. Early on a Bank Holiday Monday morning in 2006 I drove to Rosslare, having been tipped off that fishing boats from Kilmore would blockade it in a row over scallop licences.

It was before 6 a.m. when I got there and the fishing boats were already outside the harbour entrance, slowly moving back and forth, tossing around in the swell as the 'white horses', the tops of the waves, rolled continuously onto the shore.

At the ferry terminal there was the usual degree of apparent chaos when services are stopped – ships can't enter or leave and passengers find their journeys cancelled. Container lorries going to and from Britain and the continent all come to a halt and, quite quickly, a backlog grows.

With a cameraman, I was busy recording for television news, when a protest force of fishing families arrived down the slip road from the main Rosslare road and swung a lorry across it. No way back up the road and our camera car was inside the blockade. No way out to get pictures back for the news bulletin.

Appeals to the blockade didn't work. A shouting match ensued between myself and some of the protesters. They were not happy with us and would not let us through, despite my pointing out that as a result they would not get the coverage they wanted.

There was no resolution until an official from the regional fishermen's organisation arrived. Of such are news stories made and relations were restored with the fishermen and their families in Kilmore. Later in the day the blockade was lifted – after the nation had been told of the protest.

All of this is the cut and thrust of a journalist's life.

'Never hold grievances and, if you do disagree with somebody, be very sure of your ground because on this small island you are going to meet the same people over and over again.' One of my early mentoring news editors told me this and it is a piece of advice which I have never forgotten, along with the three principle assets a journalist needs:

1. The craftiness of a fox
   (to outwit rivals and find the truth of a story!)
2. The hide of a rhinoceros
   (to withstand the insults hurled at you when people are not pleased with your reportage)
3. The patience of a donkey
   (for waiting outside all the doors closed in your face!)

Rosslare also has a proud lifeboat tradition and I was there in the harbour at a very special moment in July 2004 when Coxswain Brendan Pitt spun his new charge, the seventeen-metre Severn Class lifeboat, *Donald and Barbara Broadhead*, in her own length as she turned to face the Arun Class lifeboat which she was replacing at the station. They were accompanied, line abreast, by the Kilmore Quay lifeboat, stationed to the north, and the Wexford Inshore lifeboat. Together with a fleet of local boats, they had had escorted the new lifeboat from Tuskar Rock to her future home base, on her maiden voyage from the builders.

It was one of those seafaring moments when I felt an emotional warmth towards those who risk their own lives to save those in danger on the sea, a moment when tears of joy and pleasure could well up within you, watching lifeboat crews salute each other, comrades of the sea.

I thought of how they so easily wear that responsibility: at any time, they can get called out in any weather to help those in trouble, a call for help that always gets answered.

The new lifeboat remained in position for a few minutes, saluting the former one, which had carried out many rescues, as it left for the last time from Rosslare. Then the *Donald and Barbara Broadhead* swung again in another circle and manoeuvred into the lifeboat pen.

Rosslare is an important strategic location for a lifeboat and there is great pride in the town that the RNLI service to seafarers has been carried out for many years. The Rosslare Hotel has a mini-museum collection of artefacts, memorabilia and information about the lifeboat. Its story includes legendary figures like Dick Walsh, the coxswain who led the lifeboat crew in the famous rescue of the crew of the tanker, the *World Concord*, which broke apart in heavy gales in the Irish Sea in 1954.

Dick and his crew literally chased the accommodation area of the tanker as it was blown down the Irish Sea.

'It was a fierce night and there were pieces of metal sticking out all over the accommodation area as it was tossed about in the seas. During the dark hours we followed it and I wouldn't have liked to have had to get into her in the dark with all that metal sticking out,' he recalled of the rescue.

At first light the Rosslare men moved in. The helicopter cover of today was not available and they were the only hope for those aboard the remains of the tanker. With the skill born of years at sea, Dick took his boat in time and again and they got the crew off, calling at them to come down a ladder on the outside of the heaving accommodation section. Then, as the wave lifted the lifeboat into the ship, lifeboatmen on the bow grabbed the crewman and pulled him off.

'But the last man down was the captain and there was no one left above to tell him when to turn around off the ladder and face the lifeboat to jump as we came in. We tried and he wouldn't or couldn't jump. We tried again and he didn't. Then we tried again and a brother of mine up on the bow of the lifeboat grabbed the captain by the legs and dragged him off and that ended that.'

That is a great story of the dedication and ability of lifeboatmen and their reaction in a crisis.

'The poor guys, they had been through a terrible time after their ship got into trouble and then stuck in the accommodation section as it was blown around. We got them below in the lifeboat and looked after them, but they were all seasick. Imagine that: after all their difficulties, they got sick when they were safe!'

Behind the lifeboat crews are great volunteers, particularly fundraisers. I met one of them that day in Rosslare when the new boat arrived, who had raised €50,000. She was June Ellard from Carne, further along the Wexford coast and well respected by the lifeboat crew, who go to sea thanks to her dedicated fundraising. June was delighted to be invited aboard the new boat and to see for herself what her voluntary work provides. It shows that we can all be members of the 'family of the sea'.

19

THE AQUATIC CANARIES
OF BURRISHOOLE

'Just like the canaries of old when they were used to test the air in the mines, we are testing the waters in the Atlantic and salmon are telling us about climate change and global warming.' I have always remembered those words since Ken Whelan told them to me at a lovely, picturesque, quiet and peaceful spot in County Mayo, a few miles from Newport, overlooking lovely Clew Bay. Ken is one of Ireland's top scientists, a man who has achieved a lot of respect for his dedicated work over many years. He has a strong reputation both in Ireland and abroad and he was speaking to me as director of Aquaculture and Catchment Services at the Marine Institute. We were in Burrishoole, at the Salmon Research Trust Centre, the work of which we were featuring in an edition of *Seascapes*.

The programme itself brought me one of the great experiences of radio. We were broadcasting live from the centre of Newport town and outside in the street we could see people as they stood in the pleasant evening, at the doors of pubs, shops and houses. They were listening in on transistor radios via a satellite many thousands of miles away in the skies, then back down to earthbound transmitters, and from them via RTÉ headquarters in Dublin to radio receivers around the nation, some of them on the street of Newport. Radio is marvellous!

Burrishoole nestles amongst the valleys and hills outside Newport, where scientists spend their days studying salmon and ranching them. Many of the scientific facts established there are fed into the mix of information upon which fishing quotas, fishing effort, licensing arrangements and other regulations are based. But there is a lot more to the work of the centre. The equivalent of 'aquatic canaries' was how Ken Whelan colourfully described their salmon research work.

Salmon, the 'lordly' fish, has caused more emotion and controversy than most other species. The imposition of the drift-net ban came after a lot of controversy and, despite compensation paid out by the government, it is still bitterly resented on many parts of the coast where it wiped out a centuries long tradition. Commercial fishermen viewed the ban as the government giving in to rich 'riparian' owners, who possess the fishing rights on rivers, some of them descended from ancestors who achieved these rights by conquest. However, there are also clubs, in which more 'ordinary' people are members, who own rights and, in order to preserve the species, regulations controlling salmon fishing have also been imposed on rivers.

'The information which we gain here at Burrishoole is obtained from the movements of salmon across the Atlantic Ocean,' Ken Whelan told me. 'Just like the canaries of old used to test atmosphere and safety in the mines, salmon are doing a similar type of job in the Atlantic. They are invaluable in helping the study of climate change and global warming.'

I learned a lot about the work of the Research Trust which, when we were there, was marking the founding of this unique place back in 1955. That happened through the commitment of the then board of directors of Guinness and the company's managing director at the time, Sir Hugh Beaver. Their main interest may have been sales of their alcoholic beverage and the profits to be acquired from it, but they were interested in angling and the future of salmon. They had a great ally in the then scientific advisor to the Minister for Fisheries, Dr Arthur Went. Burrishoole is testimony to the foresight that was shown so many years ago when it was acquired and became a research centre.

A map of Ireland or a coastal chart shows how ideally situated the Burrishoole system is on the track the salmon follow in the Atlantic. The programme of work there involves studying the spawning of young salmon from fish which are then released into the Atlantic. Through the amazing desire and ability of the salmon to return to the place where it was spawned, itself to spawn, they pass again through the Burrishoole system, where they are counted and selected fish are examined and studied individually.

'Salmon are a great fish which provide valuable information on their movements to us as we study them. They are an indicator of what is happening in the Gulf Stream on which Ireland is so dependent.'

The location of Burrishoole is at the eastern end of the Gulf Stream and the southernmost temperature limit of commercial fishery species such as salmon and cod. Ireland is considered internationally to be an ideal observatory location to study the implications of climate change on and through the marine environment which impacts on land, because there is more ocean in the world than earth.

From Newport a network of research has radiated out which includes the involvement of the laboratory and the scientific staff there in major European climate research initiatives, in programmes such as 'Reflect' and 'Clime'. There is collaboration with Trinity College, Dublin, and other partners from ten countries. Scientists at the Marine Institute's laboratory at Burrishoole are also investigating the effects that climate change is having on rivers and lakes and their dynamics across Europe.

Long-term monitoring involves major commitment and can be quite expensive, so the allocation of resources is essential. The Newport Centre is unique in Europe, though there is not a lot of public awareness about it or knowledge of it. Burrishoole offers great scope for research into climate change and while the public may not know a lot about it, its relevance is considerable. The work there highlights just how important salmon are to our human species.

20

FROM DUBLIN TO CORK
AND BACK AGAIN

I always find it a great pleasure when dedicated attention is paid to an old vessel and it is successfully refurbished and brought once again to life. So it was a delight to stand on the deck of the old liner tender, *Cill Áirne*, in Cork Dockyard at Rushbrooke, when she was re-launched after extensive renovation work had been carried out under the auspices of the Irish Ship & Barge Fabrication Company of Dublin. This company bought the vessel after years of her lying unused alongside the Custom House Quay in Cork City since she had become unsuitable for the tutorial work of the National Maritime College, which trains mariners for careers at sea as merchant navy officers.

The *Cill Áirne* and a sister ship, the *Blárna*, which having also done tender service duty to the liners arriving in Cork harbour, went to the Great Lakes in Canada, were the last ships to be built at the Liffey Dockyards in Dublin in 1962. They were the last riveted ships to be built in Europe. The *Cill Áirne* is 150 feet long, has a forty-foot beam and was launched in February 1963. She had famous Crossley diesel engines, which have been a delight to the many trainee marine engineers who learned their craft aboard her.

The *Cill Áirne* boarded passengers at the Deepwater Quay in Cobh and would sail out past the two forts, Carlisle and Camden, guarding the entrance to the harbour, past Roche's Point lighthouse to where the liners, too big to enter the harbour, would wait. There she would offload passengers and mail; other passengers would embark and she would bring her new cargo of humans back to Cobh for their entry to Ireland. It was the era before transatlantic air travel, when travel was luxurious and less hurried. Among the many famous people carried aboard the *Cill Áirne* were Dwight D. Eisenhower, the famous Second World War general and later American President, those great comedians of the black-and-white film era, Laurel and Hardy, and many others.

'You are looking at a two-and-a-half million euro project,' Sam Corbett of the company told me at the dockyard as the tender was pulled from dry dock No. 2, where she had just been re-launched, around to a fitting-out berth for further work. In her new livery of a black-and-red funnel, emblazoned with the ISBF house flag emblem and white upper topsides, above the black hull and red waterline she looked impressive. Two tugs moved this venerable old 'lady of Cork harbour', whose historic connections with the Lee are strong. Several mariners, who in their time had sailed aboard her, including some who learned their sea-going profession on the vessel, were at the re-launching ceremony.

'Some people in Cork have told me that they lament the loss of the *Cill Áirne* to the city, but Dublin people don't realise the shipbuilding heritage on the Liffey, so we are in a sense stepping from one to the other with the intention of preserving this vessel,' Sam Corbett said. 'Our renovation is a national maritime project in many ways, because we didn't want to see the *Cill Áirne* lost as a maritime treasure, which is what she is.'

The slogan of the Irish Ship & Barge Fabrication Company is 'Passion floats our boats' and indeed, that is required to carry out the extensive project. Boat renovation consumes money very quickly. The vessel is the only surviving serviceable ship still in the country built by Liffey Dockyard in Dublin. The intensive restoration programme, carried out in accordance with Department of the Marine regulations, has brought the vessel up beyond her original Class 5 to Class 4 passenger vessel certification, licensed to carry three hundred passengers.

After the tender serviced liners from the United States, it was the training vessel for the National Maritime College. When it could no longer meet operational regulations, it lay disused alongside the Cork Port Company's quayside. Then in stepped the Irish Ship & Barge Fabrication Company from Dublin. From Rushbrooke she was taken to the boatyard of Liam Hegarty at Oldcourt near Skibbereen in West Cork, where she was re-decked and her wood restored beautifully.

Sam Corbett and his project backers had the misfortune of a fire aboard during the renovation work at Rushbrooke, but even that setback did not deter them. 'There have been a few ports where renovation projects started and didn't finish. This one will'. They deserve to succeed.

'Rest assured, she will be well maintained and cared for in the future. We expect her to have a long future ahead of her,' Sam Corbett told me. The *Cill Áirne* is now a bar/bistro and restaurant on the fast-developing north quays of Dublin City, moored on the North Wall, near where the tall ship, *Jeanie Johnston*, is also often moored. Maritime life is reawakening on those quaysides.

21

THE BARNA BOG BOAT
AN AMAZING BOAT — OVER 5,000 YEARS OLD

To look at a boat that was nearly 6,000 years old was an amazing experience for me and somewhat humbling also. I tried to imagine what they were like, those people who were amongst the first to have made their way to the western coastline. I was humbled to realise how much we humans are merely passing through life in this world. Despite all the advances of humanity, of the human brain, we may last a hundred years at most, if we are lucky; yet a piece of wood could last nearly 6,000 years. What immense history it had been through. What had happened around it, how had life changed? People had lived, died, yet this boat, this piece of wood, continued to exist and still does, giving strong indications of how our forbears lived, the Neolithic people back in the early dawn of time in Irish history.

These ancestors of ours, perhaps the first Irish people, made this boat from a pine tree cut down about 5,500 years ago in a forest on the Galway coast.

To imagine that it all happened in an area around Barna, part of the Western Gaeltacht, where it was used, where our ancestors paddled around in it, making contact with other inhabited areas, was even more amazing to me. I stood on the beach at Barna, looking over the muddy area where the boat had been found, trying to imagine what life was like at that time. For how could the mind, dictated by modern times, appreciate that I was standing on the edge of what is now Galway Bay, but was then an inland lake.

The finding of the Barna Bog Boat, so called because of the boggy area in which it was found, proves that Galway did not have a bay over 5,000 years ago and that the present bay was created by huge levels of coastal erosion.

On the promenade at Salthill, that lovely stretch of walkway that curves around the edge of the foreshore all the way out from the legendary Claddagh, where the famous Galway hookers, the boats of Connemara, laid their historic maritime record, I marvelled at the enthusiasm of a man of intelligence, dedication and study, who bristled and seemed to bounce with the vigour and enthusiasm of his research. Professor Michael O'Connell of the National University in Galway is a man of huge commitment to his work.

'It is a find of huge archaeological, historical and social importance. It shows that this vast area,' he said, waving his hand out towards Galway Bay and across to the coastline of Clare, 'did not exist when this boat was used. This was inland; there was a lake in from the sea; it was totally different. It shows how the coast has been eroded and how much this has happened.

'These people, our forbears, they cut down pine trees to build this boat, to use it to visit other areas that were inhabited. Pine could last longer than ash and this has lasted – imagine it as you look at it – between five and six thousand years. Can you imagine that? Do you realise the importance of this, of what has been found?

'There were forests – it was a different time of climate – there were storms of a different kind. This is a most exciting discovery, of course I am excited about it,' he told me as we stood outside the national aquarium at Salthill, where the bog boat is on display.

'To have spent so many years researching, studying, to find that the evidence of life centuries, generations, ago, is there on our foreshore, this is marvellously exciting, this is of huge importance.'

Large tracts of land were eaten away as the sea worked its way in. The canoe, dug-out, or 'bog boat' as it has become popularly known, was found in December 2002 when, after a series of coastal storms, Brian and Ronán Ó Carra were looking along the beach near Barna at low tide to see if anything unusual had been exposed by the wave action.

They had previously come across other 'finds' – deer antlers amongst them and seemingly many uprooted trees – all of which gave scientific researchers indications about the lifestyle of our forbears.

The boat was recovered with great care and taken to the National Aquarium at Salthill, where Liam Twomey and his staff protected it, under the guidance of the National Museum. The museum has since allowed it to be placed on permanent exhibition there, in a specially constructed pool which provides continuous water circulation and which is laid out to give an indication of what the Galway coastline out towards Barna may have looked like nearly 6,000 years ago.

I have done many stories for *Seascapes*, but there are times when I have stood in awe of what I have seen, when I have tried to imagine the original scene of what is now before my eyes. To imagine that the remains of the boat I was looking at could be as old as the Pyramids, that I found awe-inspiring. Professor Conor Newman, also of the National University at Galway, has studied many 'bog boat' or 'canoe' discoveries, of which a total of around 350 have been made in Ireland.

Try to imagine one of these vessels being used to carry the exalted personage of a papal nuncio who was angry about this method of transport. Professor Newman told me a lovely story about the papal nuncio to Ireland in 1516 being taken on one of these dugout canoes to Lough Derg, for which he was charged a penny. The nuncio was none-too-happy, either with the fee or the condition of the boat, which he apparently considered dirty and dangerous! He made his views forcibly known to all those with whom he came in contact, not apparently thinking much of the Irish or their maritime transport system to his prayerful ministrations on his visit to Lough Derg.

The largest dugout canoe found in Ireland is known as the 'Lurgan logboat', which was also discovered in Galway – at Addergoole Bog near Tuam and measures 15.25 metres in length. It was made from the trunk of an oak tree, believed to have been cut down around 2,500 BC. This is displayed in the National Museum in Dublin.

It takes skill and balance not to capsize a dugout canoe, but interestingly there are no general indications that Irish versions were ever made with outriggers to give extra stability. One exception was found at Gormanstown in County Meath. It had holes drilled along the gunwales, believed to have been for outriggers. Despite canoes being found, paddles to propel them have rarely been located. For propulsion the most common item used seems to have been perforated lengths of ashwood, a few of which have been located.

22

FISH ARE NOT STUPID
– THEY LIKE MUSIC

Some of the more interesting debates I have been involved in during my twenty years presenting *Seascapes* concern whether fish can feel pain and if they have brains. I was told as a youngster that to eat fish would give you brains. These days fish have been found to be a very healthy diet, particularly for the Omega 3 found in the more oily fish.

I've interviewed quite a few scientists over the years, discussing what happens when a hook sticks in the mouth of a fish or what fish feel when an angler hits a fish to kill it. Some scientists claimed that fish did suffer pain, others contradicted that. However, when I talked to Dr Culum Browne from Macquarie University in Sydney, Australia, on the programme, we had a debate about whether fish were stupid, or if they had brains and a form of understanding. A biology lecturer, he maintained that fish are actually quite clever.

'They are schooled in survival skills and those in the wild can even teach their peer, raised in captivity, how to get by in the sea. ... Fish are not the bowl-circling dimwits people imagine them to be. They could be as socially able as monkeys and elephants.'

During his research he put rainbow fish into a tank with a section of a trawler net that had a single hole in it. Without any previous experience of the situation and after making a few preliminary runs at the net, the fish found the escape hole. A year later, in a similar test and using the same fish, they found the hole at the first attempt!

'So they had retained the skill of finding the way out in a form of memory.'

That research work followed a study in the United States, where unusual marine research is regularly carried out and reported, which claimed that fish can recognise different types of music. The conclusions were that fish are able to distinguish sound in their own environment. At the Rowland Institute for Science in Cambridge, Massachusetts, carp were taught the difference between blues and classical music, when it was played through loudspeakers into a fish tank.

At Stanford University in California, researchers claimed that the type of reasoning known as 'transitive interference', which is naturally learned by young children as they grow up, has also been found in fish. According to Russell Fernald, a professor of biological sciences, 'they use it to figure out where they are in the social order.' Researchers claimed to have found that a tiny African fish called cichlids climb their social ladder by picking fights! During experiments in an aquarium, the researchers saw that some fish stood by and watched while others fought and the losers swam away on their own, going out of the 'social circle' of other fish.

23

THE FERRY AND A CENTURY-OLD TRADITION

Carlingford Lough is a beautiful place where I have met some very interesting people in my years of recording interviews for *Seascapes*. It has good sailing waters and you can go right back to the Newry Ship Canal. It was there that I met, interviewed and then wished *bon voyage* to two fine sailors who have put thousands of miles under the keel of their steel yacht, *Mithril*. They have been all over the world – to the Arctic wastes, to the Southern Ocean, the Caribbean, Africa.

The voyages of *Mithril* have been reported by Geraldine Foley, who sails with her partner, Peter Maxwell. They keep a careful eye on their costs, for they don't have regular jobs like the rest of the more 'ordinary' land-based humans. But they certainly enjoy their sailing and their never-ending journeys around the world, during which they have experienced good weather and bad, but *Mithril* has carried them safely

They set off from the Ship Canal in Newry and continue to cruise the world.

To drive around Carlingford Lough, where the Mountains of Mourne quite literally sweep down to the sea, is to experience spectacular scenery. Along the way I met Brendan O'Neill who was operating a ferry service from Omeath in County Louth, on the Republic's side of the lough, to Warrenpoint near Newry in County Down, on the Northern Ireland side, where I met him.

Lo and behold, he had named the ferry *Seascapes*. His company was Castle Cruises Ltd. and he was carrying on a family tradition which went back over a hundred years. He had bought a new boat in China, where it had been manufactured and it was taken by sea to Warrenpoint, where he was fitting it out for launching. He joked that people were calling his boat 'the Chinese takeaway', but he was calling it, officially, *Seascapes*, so it was the first boat to be named after the programme.

Brendan told me that there had once been twenty-eight boats providing ferry services around the lough, but his was the only one remaining. The local council in Warrenpoint has done a fine job of developing the maritime heritage of the area and it is great to see boats moored right in the centre of the town.

24

THE SUIR COTS

Sitting in a cot on the River Suir at Carrigeen in the Mooncoin area of south Kilkenny, looking across the broad expanse of the river to County Waterford, was a great experience.

Now it wasn't a cot of the kind more familiar to parents as they look after their young offspring. This was a special cot. I nearly overbalanced it because, as Buddy Kelly – in his late sixties and happily sitting in it – told me, I was more used to the easy urban life and needed a bit of a spell of getting my balance right. And there was I, mistakenly thinking that as I had sailed yachts for years, I knew a bit about balance, but it was a delicate operation getting into the small boat in its berth, a square cut out of the bank.

The Nore, Piltown and Fiddown are names more associated with the great tradition of Kilkenny hurling than with a mari-time tradition. Yet there is a huge maritime tradition around the Nore and the Suir in this part of Kilkenny, which I discovered when I drove in to Piltown and then along roads I had never even known of to arrive eventually at the banks of the Suir. I was in a place which didn't seem to me to have changed much through the centuries.

Upriver I saw a man in a small boat that was literally covered with reeds. It reminded me of something I had seen in photos of places like the Ganges in India, boats that came from the past that looked nothing like anything associated with modern life and carrying what was not much part of life today either. But in this part of Kilkenny there is careful nurturing of tradition and pride in maintaining it. It also helps maintain a skill that is dying – as is the kind of the rural countryside it maintains: that of the thatcher and the thatched roof. How does all of this relate to the boats on the Suir? The cots go out on the river to cut the reeds, bring them to the bank, stack and dry them for the thatcher. It is a part of Ireland far from those whose lives are concentrated in the artificiality of urban life. To see the cots of the Suir is to have the spirit lifted.

Buddy Kelly described to me how these special boats, the Suir cots, were used. Buddy was one of the fishermen who continue a long tradition of snap-net and draft-net fishing on the Suir. Amidst the abolition of net fishing for salmon, these fishermen, whose traditions go back centuries, must also be considered. As an island people, our maritime traditions should predominate in national culture. The cots are long, narrow boats berthed in cuts made into the riverbank at Carrigeen and are also used to gather reeds from the riverbank. Watching one of them come down the river loaded with reeds was a very special thing to see. There is even a fishing language with words like dag, cippín, smacthtín and others having a meaning not understood outside the area.

So I tried out the cláirín, the board fitted at the stern of the cot as the seat for the snap-net fisherman. I found that a sense of balance is important to keep the cot upright, but Buddy had no such problem. In years past, the cot fishermen of the Suir were much in demand to go to Newfoundland, where their skills were greatly valued.

Indeed, I met a fisherman in Newfoundland, down the coast from St John's, the capital, when I was there. It was in an 'outpost', as these small fishing villages are called, and when I began to interview him he had an accent which I identified as Waterford – and it was. But when I asked him what part of the Decies he came from, he told me had never been in Waterford. He was the fourth generation of Newfoundlanders whose ancestors had come from Waterford. The accent survived all that time, but over there was counted as a Newfoundland accent.

I went to Carrigeen to find out more about the boats, cots, punts and wherries of the Suir after reading Coracle Press' production of a book by Thomas Cuddihy of Piltown, who built many cots. It reproduced his notes and designs. As well as being used for fishing, his boats were raced in regattas on the Suir, and *Island Maid* was one of the most successful. The Cuddihy family has maintained his workshop at their home in Piltown, which led me, microphone in hand, to hear more and to see this treasure of old boatbuilding tools and skills.

In the shed, Tom Cuddihy talked to me about his boatbuilding grandfather. A local man, Joe Sullivan, had written a book about this area of South Kilkenny, *To School by the Banks*, which recorded that in the early roll books of the schools in the area, 'fisherman' was one of the most prominent occupations of the parents.

Buddy Kelly was proud of being a snap-net fisherman and told me about the skill of the men who used a paddle in one hand to move the boat, and the net in the other to catch fish, all the time maintaining their balance in what seemed to me a fairly difficult and, for myself, perilous situation, but not to Buddy and his colleagues.

Buddy had come back from London, to where he had emigrated as so many had to do to earn a living, in order to go fishing on the river and maintain the tradition of his family. He retained a great belief in the fishery, though the number of salmon had decreased on the river over the years, as had the catches he was taking. We talked about the attitude of anglers, environmentalists, politicians, the fishing authorities and the public towards commercial salmon netsmen, and Buddy was in no doubt that the authorities would prefer to see the end of the man who makes his living from the river.

'They want us out. That's the way it is. But why is all the talk about the fish that the commercial man takes? We don't take a lot in our boats. There are the problems with the drift-netters, then there is the catches which the anglers themselves take and nobody seems to want to talk much about pollution and what the housing developments are doing to the spawning beds and to the river itself. There are problems, no doubt about that, but it is easy to point the finger at the commercial men and ignore all the other problems.

'For example, there's the pollution. I'm disgusted by what I see in the way the river is being polluted. There's all sorts of things being put into it and those who are quick to condemn the way fishermen make their living conveniently overlook all the other damage that is being done. The people who live in the towns, they throw their rubbish into it, they put their washing liquids down the shores, they don't care and then there are others who take the gravel and want to use it for building. It disgusts me that they don't care what damage they do to the rivers, but they blame the man who takes a few salmon to earn a living for himself.'

In the time of Thomas Cuddihy it was different. Then the River Suir was a lifeline to many families in the area, who depended on the salmon fishing. Thomas was a fine boat builder and a fisherman on the Suir and carried on the craft of building fishing cots, punts and racing cots. He raced in many regattas which were a popular pastime on the river and became champion of the Suir, Nore and Barrow at the People's Regatta in Waterford in 1909–1910. His famous racing cot which won many a race was known as the *Island Maid*.

In too much of Irish life our traditions are being killed off and too often it is the power and the money of others who are the cause.

It was good to sit in a cot and talk about boats and the pride of fishing with a man who has an obvious pride in his craft. He talked a lot of common sense. There is a tradition in what the salmon fishermen of the Suir do and they are as entitled to continue to make a living, surely, as the anglers are to demand that there should be more fish available for them. It all points to the need to talk, discuss and jointly plan for the future without confrontation. I have taken a lot of calls about the salmon issue, ever since it was made clear that the government is not going to buy out entirely all salmon netting licences.

On the banks of the Suir that Saturday afternoon near Carrigeen I also watched the cots being used to bring reeds ashore for thatching, another example of the uses to which the boats are put. Originally they were doubled-ended and narrower, but they have been adapted – they now have more width, a blunt stern for the use of outboard engines and more space on board for two men to work the boat.

South Kilkenny is noted for the number of clustered farm villages and the number of thatched roofs which still predominate. Because of its location this area has been influenced by the Suir, one of Ireland's great waterways. Fishing is a tradition in this area and, before any action or decision is taken which wipes it out, a lot of consideration has to be given to how important it is to maintain tradition in rural areas. The boats have their own cut-out areas for berthing and as Joe Sullivan, who has written a book about the history of the area, told me: 'It is one of the last great traditions still carried on and deserves to be respected and protected.'

The fishermen developed a language with words of their own in this area, 'dag,' 'ledge,' 'scar,' are words that I was told you would have to be a native fisherman to understand.

But one thing it was easy to understand – traditional fishing deserves more than criticism, it deserves to be preserved.

25

FROM POLAND TO THE GREAT ISLAND TO BUILD BOATS

Immigration to Ireland from Poland has become more common in recent years, but there are not too many Polish people who decided to settle in Ireland then built boats to make a living because they felt they could make better ones than they were using in their work.

Frank Kowalski is of Polish-Irish extraction and first came to Cork at the age of twenty-four, to grow oysters near East Ferry at the back of the Great Island in Cork harbour. But he found that only provided a living for part of the year, so something else was needed and he tried angling charters. The boats he used didn't satisfy him, so he began to think of designing and building his own. Having learned naval architecture and boat-building techniques, he set about doing so.

It was at the back of his house that I met him, overlooking a lovely stretch of water near East Ferry at the back of Great Island. This is an actual island, where thousands of people live, but whose sole connection with the mainland of Cork is a single hump-back bridge at Belvelly.

Frank created a good business for himself and I met him in sheds close to his home.

'Boat building is a demanding craft and you exist by the quality of what you produce. We do it all here ourselves and, so far, the response is good.'

I spent a few days at his yard, watching the process of designing and building. Frank says he is the only builder left in Ireland constructing workboats from the basic idea to the finished product. It is intriguing to see a boat taken from the mould – almost the birth of the product that was first fashioned in the eye of the designer. He developed a catamaran for sea angling amongst other designs and productions. He named his company Safehaven – rather appropriate for the beautiful area around East Ferry.

Boats for use as island ferries in Scotland and Ireland and for angling off the English coast are amongst Safehaven's successful productions. When I talked to him he was planning production of a new twenty-eight-foot leisure boat, to be built at an additional factory at Little Island, further up Cork harbour.

26

THE ROCK OF MISERY AND A CHANCE FOR MARRIAGE

Keep off, keep off, good ship from me,
For I am the rock of misery.

These are the words attributed to a man who cannot speak and who remains forever pointing to tragedy. He is atop a pillar and is said to chant the words when the wind howls around the pillar, which is estimated at about forty feet high. As the ground is uneven, it makes it a bit difficult to hop around barefoot.

And why would anyone want to do that?

It's the tradition that if a woman hops barefooted all around the pillar three times, she will be married within the year, presuming that is her desire of course!

There are unusual landscapes and seascapes around the coast and this is certainly one of them. Three miles across Tramore Bay is another pillar, but without a man atop, at Brownstown Head.

The pillars were erected in 1823 after a disaster seven years earlier in January 1816, when 363 men, women and children were drowned. They were aboard a ship, the *Seahorse*, driven ashore in Tramore Bay during a gale. Apparently, at least some of the money for the work had to be raised by the families of those who died.

Tramore can be a difficult and dangerous bay to enter, particularly for a vessel without engine power. A ship could become 'embayed', unable to make its way out, and this apparently happened to the *Seahorse*. It is also believed that she mistook the entrance to Tramore for that of the safer Waterford harbour, three miles further east of Brownstown. By the time the crew realised their mistake, it was too late. There have been 122 sea disasters in Tramore Bay over the years.

'The Metal Man', erected in 1823, is still standing and I can claim to have helped get him repainted and restored. I was asked to give publicity to local attempts which had been going on for some time, but were bogged down in disagreement with the landowner on whose fields the Metal Man stands and who had sealed off public access. Local interests had offered to pay for the paint and the work, but there were problems with access, insurance and so on. After the story was reported on *Seascapes*, the difficulties were overcome and the Metal Man, a figure of a seaman in the naval rig of the 1800s, got a new 'coat' and some remedial work to his pointing finger.

The first owners of the Metal Man were the marine insurers, Lloyds of London, who held it for over a hundred years. Then, when war raged in Europe, the Irish Lights in Dublin took over ownership. After that, when electronics provided better navigational warnings, the Metal Man ceased to get attention. He is thought to be the work of Thomas Kirk, who is also believed to have carved the statue of Lord Nelson which used to stand in O'Connell Street in Dublin, before it was blown up by Republicans.

Researching the story I came across another metal man who had been made at the same time as the Tramore one and stands off Strandhill at the entrance to Sligo harbour. I was told there had been a third man, but he may have fallen off a ship carrying them to Ireland. While his two companions warn of dangers for shipping, it seems his safety was not so assured!

27

THE COBH MAN WHO GAVE A MOUNTAIN TO THE ANTARCTIC

A letter from a committee in Cobh took me to a graveyard in the town to read the name of a man I had not known about, whose memory had been forgotten by many, despite his great courage.

The names of the great Antarctic explorers are well known – Scott, Shackleton, Amundsen, Tom Crean from Kerry and others – but I hadn't heard before of Robert Forde from Cobh, a man who had been known in that town for many years as the man who had frostbite. Cobh people remembered him around the town for his frostbitten, damaged hands, which were regularly bandaged, many years after he had been in the polar regions.

The letter came from a committee which had taken upon itself the task of erecting a memorial to him. His journey to Antarctica a century before has left its mark, as the 4,000-foot Mount Forde is named after him. In the Old Church Cemetery at Cobh the gravestone to him has only a brief reference to his exploration of the Polar regions – *With Capt. Scott, B.A. EX 1910/13.*

Robert Forde was born on 29 August 1875 in Cork and joined the Royal Navy at the age of sixteen when he had grown to 5 foot

8 inches, according to the records, which described him as having 'hazel eyes, dark brown hair and a fresh complexion'. Two years later he had signed on for a twelve-year stint in the navy, where he was rated as 'Ordinary Seaman', having started out as 'Boy 2nd Class'. He served on several ships and was promoted to 'Petty Officer 2nd Class' in 1902 and promoted again to 1st Class by 1904.

Like many Irish seafarers, he volunteered for the British Antarctic Expedition in 1910 at a time of great interest in polar exploration, when it was the pinnacle of a sailor's ambition. Explorers were highly regarded, seen as heroes, members of an elite. Thousands applied, few were chosen.

Listed as having an address at 52 Harbour Row, Queenstown, then the name of Cobh, Forde was aged thirty-five when he was appointed to the *Terra Nova*, the legendary exploration ship, with the rank of petty officer on 30 May 1910. There was another Corkman on that expedition, Patrick Keohane, and both were involved in establishing Captain Robert Falcon Scott's 'Corner Camp', thirty-five miles from what was known as Cape Evans. It was tough going and a lot of hardship was suffered.

Forde was in a group of thirteen who headed out from Cape Evans in January 1911 to explore the polar cap, aware that they were chosen from eight thousand who had applied to go. It was hard and demanding, exceptionally tiring, and sleep was difficult. Men had to haul sledges because the ponies that had been taken on the expedition were not suitable for the area in which they were trying to advance. They were also hit by blizzards as they marched across the ice. Also in the group were Lt Evans, Tom Crean, Keohane and others whose names are written in polar history.

At one point, because of Scott's concern about the ponies, Evans, Forde and Keohane were ordered to go back on their tracks with the animals, while the rest of the party advanced. When the group reassembled, a few ponies had died and some of the party could not be found. There was also no contact with the *Terra Nova*. Eventually the difficulties were sorted out and the members of the expedition party made contact with each other, but then blinding snowdrifts hit their camp. Temperatures plummeted as low as -40°C and Forde suffered severely frostbitten hands.

By March 1912 he was suffering so badly that he was ordered back to the ship and, aboard the *Terra Nova*, skilful medical treatment saved his hands. He was invalided back to New Zealand after a month. Captain Scott said that the loss of Forde to the expedition was a serious blow and wrote in his log that he had 'no one who could replace him'.

Forde was promoted to chief petty officer for his courage and commitment to the expedition and, on return to England, was assigned to *HMS Vivid* in October 1913. When the First World War broke out the following year, Forde served in several ships and remained in the Royal Navy until he was demobilised.

Then Robert Forde returned to Queenstown where he retired and lived on his British naval pension at Harbour Row, overlooking Cork harbour, with two sisters – Susan and Sarah. He never married and is not recorded as having taken up any local employment. Older Cobh people recalled seeing 'his hands bandaged or otherwise covered so that his frostbitten hands were not seen'. He died in his home town on 13 March 1959, where a memorial committee has been raising funds to erect a memorial to him. The seafaring man whose name is recalled on Mount Forde in Antarctica deserves no less.

28

A SPECIAL GARDEN

I am not a particularly good gardener, but on the eastern approach to the fishing port of Castletownbere, deep in the heart of the West Cork countryside, for which I have a particular *grá* (that beautiful Irish word for love) is the Locmiquelic Garden. Driving into the port, you pass it on the right-hand side of the road, just after passing the bridge to Dinish Island. That is an island that was designated as a fish industry processing plant, where once I stood watching fishermen blockade the island in protest against national fishing policies. It is also an island where a major Spanish fishing company promised hundreds of jobs, got grants from the Industrial Development Authority and several Irish fishing licences for Spanish boats before closing the factory and throwing the local Irish out of their jobs. I often wondered if the government ever learned the lesson about the importance of fishing, to me it doesn't seem that they ever did.

But let us get back to the garden, which is at the entrance to Castletownbere. It is dominated by an anchor which is believed to have come from the ship on which Wolfe Tone sailed during the ill-fated French expedition to Bantry Bay in 1796. The history of the anchor is shrouded in the mists of time, but it has been identified as a French anchor from a ship which anchored in Bantry Bay, preparatory to an intended invasion.

Confirmation of its origin comes through a journal from that time by Edward Morgan, who recorded a French fleet anchored off Bank harbour on the northern side of Berehaven harbour, not far from Ahabeg, where the anchor was found. Tradition has it that because of bad weather, French vessels in the harbour cut their cables and left their anchors behind when they proceeded to sea in an attempt to ride out the severe gales which struck the invasion fleet.

The anchor was found in 1994 by two divers – Liam Salmon and Frank Hanley – while repairing a salmon cage at a fish farming area. It was almost completely buried in mud and leaning towards the north-west. The letters 'IND' were inscribed on the top of the shank and that led some historians to believe it was the anchor from the ship, *L'Indomptable*, which Wolfe Tone was aboard.

Following examination by the National Museum of Ireland the anchor was presented to the Beara Historical Society which had it refurbished by John Tim O'Sullivan and Denis O'Driscoll. It was then displayed at the Locmiquelic Garden, named after the French town in Brittany, with which Castletownbere is twinned. The twinning took place in 1986/87 after a group from Brittany on a walking tour of Ireland visited here.

If you are driving into Castletownbere, stop for a moment and walk into the garden. There is a sense of tranquillity, of a certain degree of peace, even though it is only yards from the busy roadway. Think of how Irish history could have been changed if the French expedition and Wolfe Tone, who came within sight of Bantry, had managed to land. The weather defeated them.

Weather is such a vital part of life on this small island on the periphery of Europe. Think of how those who run our national life have failed to grasp that single, most vital aspect of our culture, our very being. We are an island people, but where is the national pride at government level in being islanders?

Sadly missing, I think.

29

FOUR HUNDRED DIED TO BUILD DÚN LAOGHAIRE HARBOUR

Dublin bay has a long shoreline, much of which can be enjoyed riding the DART – Dublin Area Rapid Transport train – from Howth around the bay and down as far as Greystones, which lies over the county boundary in County Wicklow and where the foreshore is being developed after considerable disagreement over planning and the environment.

Along that shoreline there is a reminder of how stark, frightening and destructive the coast, which appears so beautiful and tranquil on a pleasant summer's day, can be when bad weather arrives. What amazed me on the day when people gathered to remember a terrible tragedy that occurred here in 1807 was the huge rainbow which appeared in the sky as the commemoration ended and appeared to almost form an archway over the area of tragedy. With its beautiful, magnificent kaleidoscope of colours it seemed, to my imagination, almost to be an archway for the souls of those lost on a horrific day in Dublin Bay through which to finally enter another world of peace and tranquillity. This happened as the people of today acknowledged their loss and so brought closure to a tragic story in Irish maritime history.

That commemoration took place in howling winds and lashing rain, as the seas seemed to throw themselves in fury onto the shore close to where those remembering the dead had gathered. Were those same waves furiously spending themselves to tell us that we would never succeed when the awesome power of the sea decided to spurn mere mortals who died in fear and terror?

It was 18 November 1807 when two sailing ships left Pigeon House harbour in Dublin. The *Prince of Wales* and the *Rochdale* were transport vessels and they were carrying soldiers, and their families, who had volunteered for foreign service to fight the armies of Napoleon, then rampaging through Europe. They had been offered more money and better conditions, even the prospect of other rewards if they went. In those days, families often travelled with the troops as they might have nowhere else to live during the long absence of the breadwinners.

Volunteers had been sought from the Irish militia regiments and those aboard had responded from places as far away as Cork. It was a time when travel to Dublin was arduous, long and difficult and many would have walked part of the way to Dublin, because soldiers' families would not have had much money and there was no system at that time for transporting dependants, whatever about the serving soldiery.

In those days, once a ship left the safety of the port, which ended at the Pigeon House, there was nowhere to go for shelter in adverse weather conditions. As the soldiers and their families boarded the ships in weather that showed every sign of worsening, with gales driving sleet into the bay, the scene was being set for an awful tragedy, the only positive outcome of which would be the building of Dún Laoghaire harbour.

The two ships were not the only ones which left the Pigeon House on 18 November. Others did also but managed to sail clear. The *Prince of Wales* and the *Rochdale* were no bigger than large modern fishing trawlers, small compared to modern-day passenger ships. The *Prince of Wales* was a sloop of 103 tons with a draught of 11 feet, under a 100 feet long, built in Cheshire in 1787. The *Rochdale* was larger than the *Prince of Wales*, built in 1797, a brig of 135 tons, with a ten-foot draught and about 130 feet long.

Soon after the ships cast off their shore lines, a snowstorm set in, driven by an increasing easterly gale, which was getting violent as it kicked up the sea, and big waves were driven into Dublin Bay. The ships had sailed with the tide and were observed trying to make their way out of the bay as night drew in and a cloak of darkness covered the water. In occasional breaks from the snowstorm, lights could be seen from the shore, as the ships battled to get clear into deeper water away from the dangers of the shoreline. Those watching from the shore must have wondered just what conditions those on the ships were enduring, even as they themselves hurried home to gain shelter from the worsening weather.

But the following morning, observers on shore saw that, though the ships had gained ground and were seemingly making headway outside the harbour area, they were now labouring against the violent weather and the worsening conditions in the open sea. During the day the wind rose further as the gales increased and drove snow before them. It was so thick that it shrouded the bay area at times and no one could see what was happening.

Aboard the ships a decision was made to try to anchor, but this proved futile and the anchors were lost. To observers onshore

Derrynane National Park, Co. Kerry.

A horse grazing near the coast near Derrynane, Co. Kerry.

The Cliffs of Moher rise up to 214 metres above the Atlantic Ocean.

The power of the Atlantic: waves crashing near the Burren, Co. Clare.

South coast seascape, Robert's Cove cliff walk.

The Dingle Peninsula, County Kerry: the most westerly point in Ireland.

Memorial Cross, Waterville, Co. Kerry

The tide may be out but the danger remains. Malahide, County Dublin.

Union Hall is a small port in Cork which provides safe shelter to both fishing and pleasure craft.

Galley Head Lighthouse, near Rosscarbery, Co. Cork.

Youghal Strand is one of the finest beaches on Ireland's south coast. The town of Youghal has a distinctive shape, stretched as it is along the steep bank of the river Blackwater.

it seemed that the ships had decided that they could not make safely out to sea and were trying to turn back to Dublin Port for safety. The *Prince of Wales* was the first to be driven ashore, as night again drew in. In the darkness, she hit the rocks behind Blackrock House. At that stage a longboat was launched and Captain Jones, the ship's master, with the crew, two soldiers and the wife of the ship's steward with a child, got into it and rowed away from the ship as it was pounded onto the rocks.

According to reports they 'rowed for some distance along the shore, not knowing it well enough to try to land in safety because of the conditions'. But then one of the ship's sailors fell overboard and, in terror trying to survive, found that his feet were touching the bottom. He was in shallow water and shouted out the good news for the rest of those in the longboat who ran it aground and managed to walk shore to safety. They made their way into Blackrock and shelter, but made no effort whatsoever to help those still on the ship. The 120 people aboard all died.

Meanwhile, the other ship, the *Rochdale,* was in her last throes of fighting the gale, and those aboard faced almost inevitable death. They were thrown around as the ship lifted and plunged; women were screaming; children were terrified; sails were ripped to shreds. The crew had no hope of saving their ship, though more frantic attempts were made to try to anchor and hold her against the sea conditions.

Again, these failed and, in the darkness, blue lights were burned to alert those onshore that the ship was in serious trouble. Guns were also fired by the soldiers aboard to draw attention to their plight. Several anchors were thrown out, but their cables snapped and the ship, now under bare poles – just the masts with no sails – was driven irresistibly towards the shore where death loomed. In the darkness the increasing power of the waves had the ship in their total control and swung her towards Sandy Cove. Then suddenly the ship swept past what was an old pier at Dunleary (as it was called at the time) and struck the rocks under the Martello Tower at Seapoint.

It was only half a mile from where the 120 were abandoned aboard the *Prince of Wales*. As she broke up, the passengers and crew were hit by falling spars or dragged off by the waves and drowned. Wives were torn from the grasp of their husbands; children from the despairing arms of their mothers.

There were 265 officers, crew, military officers, soldiers and their families aboard the *Rochdale*. Not one survived. When light came up the following morning, mutilated bodies were found all along the shore and over the next days more were washed up.

The tragedy caused an uproar and huge controversy. A petition was started for the building of what was described as an 'asylum harbour' at Dunleary, now Dún Laoghaire, which would provide a port of refuge in bad weather for ships in trouble. It eventually led to the building of the present Dún Laoghaire harbour.

The *Prince of Wales* struck a granite outcrop to the west of where Seapoint DART Station is now located. The jagged, granite foreshore seen today is much the same as it was when the ship struck. The *Rochdale* was driven ashore close to Seapoint's Martello Tower.

It was in that area that Dún Laoghaire–Rathdown County Council, supported by several voluntary, community organisations, arranged the commemoration ceremony on 19 November 2007, the two hundredth anniversary of the tragedy. As the weather recreated some of what had been experienced in 1807 – howling winds, lashing rain and big seas – I recalled descriptions of the time, how wreckage and bodies had been strewn along the shore of Dublin Bay 'from Ringsend to Dalkey'. Many of those who died lie buried in graveyards at Carrickbrennan, Monkstown and Merrion.

As the ceremony ended, that rainbow appeared, lighting up the grey, black sky, with the clouds sweeping past, driven by the wind. Was it an indication that, as the present-day generation commemorated the tragedy, the souls of those who died were at peace?

30

FORTY-FIVE FISHERMEN DIED IN THE NIGHT KNOWN ON THE WEST COAST AS 'THE GREAT DISASTER'

This sad disaster, nothing came faster
Being in October, we long mind the date
When those brave fishermen went out fishing
On Friday night, the twenty-eighth.
They left their homes late in the evening
About five o'clock, it was not late
But little thinking, as the stars were blinking
That they would meet with a drowning fate.

Patrick Tierney

Journalists often resort to a local hostelry to find a story – or to get more information and an additional view on what they have already been told. The Irish country pub is a place where tongues become a bit freer after pleasantries have been exchanged, your antecedents checked, your background established and the reason for you being there, a stranger in what is, in many a rural area, another 'home place' for the local customers.

It was in such a place that the opening lines to this chapter were quoted to me, the story of one village and its fishermen, lost in the biggest fishing disaster ever in Ireland. It is not particularly well known, but one village pledged never to forget the men who died and, in eighty years, has kept that promise.

Seascapes is welcomed in any coastal area to which I travel, which is at once a great satisfaction and also a humbling experience, in that I am indebted to so many people who have trusted me and told me their stories. It is also a lesson in responsibility, in that people perceive *Seascapes* as the voice of the maritime sector, as their programme and their voice.

So after my accent, my voice, was deciphered and identified at Lacken in County Mayo, I learned more about what local people call 'the West Coast Disaster', the worst single tragedy which fishermen have ever encountered in Irish history:

> *There are heart thrills of deep bitter anguish,*
> *In the homes of the fishermen brave,*
> *Who perished on the twenty-eighth of October,*
> *Beneath the Atlantic's wild wave.*
> *It shocked the whole world with its horror,*
> *When the news spread around on the day*
> *Of the awful disaster that happened*
> *In Cleggan and Lacken and poor Iniskea.*
>
> William Burns, Portacloy, Broadhaven

It takes some time and careful following of the signposts out of Ballina to get to Lacken and, if you drive into the village along the foreshore, you will come to where the road narrows and seems to go across the sand, but actually skirts around it. To your left you will see St Patrick's parish church, beside which lay, on the morning of 28 October 2007, what looked like a long rowing boat on a trailer.

There were a few men with weather-beaten faces, the faces of men who fished and who knew the sea in all her moods and elements, looking at it, feeling the wood, examining as men who know boats, the 'lines' – the shape – of the boat will. This boat was the modern version of those from which fishermen died in the worst sea tragedy to hit Lacken. The open boats have not changed a lot since 8 October 1927.

> *A violent hurricane bore down upon them,*
> *It left bones steeping and many weeping*
> *From Rossadilisk to Lacken Bay.*
>
> Patrick Tierney

When I drove into Lacken the wind was whipping up the waves and the tide was on the way in.

'You'd do best not to try driving straight across, go around the longer way, up past the church, along the hill and down to the pier that way. It would be safer,' a local man told me as I wound down the window to check directions and the rain pelted in, driven by the strong wind. 'It's not too unlike the night of the disaster, but they had driving snow as well.'

I drove the longer way around and down to Lacken Pier. It was Saturday evening, the night was drawing in. It was cold, miserable, as I took my recorder from the car and literally struggled against the wind to the water's edge. I wanted to record sound effects for the special half-hour edition of *Seascapes* we were planning to broadcast about the commemoration. It was difficult to shelter the microphone, even with its 'wind gag' – a cover to keep down the sound of the wind across the microphone – against the howling wind, as I tried also to get the sound of the waves throwing themselves against the shore onto the rocks and then receding.

Half-ways back up the hill from the pier was the memorial which local people had erected to mark the eightieth anniversary of the tragedy. I thought of that night and how men had put out in their boats to catch fish. It is what fishermen do to earn a living.

There was no indication of a gale on the afternoon of Friday, 28 October 1927, between 5 and 5.30 p.m. when the local fishermen walked the same pier, to launch their twenty-five-foot boats. Herring fishing had been exceptionally good the week before in the bay itself, so none of the nine boats which set out were going to be too far from the shore in Lacken Bay, an inlet of the much larger Killala Bay. But suddenly, the sky got very dark; so quickly it was a frightening change. The crews of the boats shouted to each other, as this was before boats had radios. Neither did they have any communication method with the shore:

On that fateful evening it was so deceiving
As they were leaving the tranquil shore
For a hard night's fishing it was their living
Those perished victims whose loss we deplore.
The storm started the crews were parted
As they bravely battled the angry sea.

Anon

Ashore, one man had run desperately to the pier to warn the men not to go out. He had a radio, one of the first in the area, and it was not easy to hear the transmissions from Radió Éireann back in Dublin. There was a lot of crackle and other noise competing with the broadcaster's voice in those early days of radio. The parish priest of Lacken, Fr Michael Quinn, had heard a gale warning on his wireless set and he tried to convey it to the fishermen. 'But they had either gone out before he reached them, or did not pay much heed to the wireless, a new gadget to them, fishermen who felt they could read the signs much better than any machine,' so local history recalls in Lacken.

Another version says: 'The priest heard the forecast and rushed from his house down to the pier. The night was dead calm at that time, but he heard a forecast of the storm on the wireless. He rushed to the pier only to find that all the boats were gone out. He told the people to get all the lamps they could gather and to light them on the pier as a warning to the fishermen. The men were out too far, it seems, to see the lights and all of a sudden, the storm burst.'

Out in the bay, the crews of the boats could barely see each other as the wind rose and lashed the waves into spray and spume that was flung into their faces. The men could no longer hear each other because of the roaring gale. They rowed in what they thought to be the direction of the pier, their eyes stinging from the salt water being flown in their faces.

Only two of the nine boats that had set out made it back to the pier. Five others were lucky that their boats were washed onto Lacken Strand, the beach which I had avoided in my car because of possible danger. The crews of these boats scrambled ashore.

But there were two others still out in the bay and they were blown towards the cliffs on the eastern side. Frantically, the fishermen tried to row their boats against the gale, but they were in trouble and desperately tried to row clear. The boat called *St*

Patrick was smashed against the rocks, but her crew managed to steady her for vital seconds to scramble onto the rocks and get ashore. They succeeded, all except one – thirty-year-old Anthony Kearney.

The *Rose of Lacken* was also smashed against the rocks and its eight crew members were drowned:

Thomas Lynott (aged 52)
Thomas Goldrick (46)
Michael Goldrick (22)
Pat Goldrick (19)
Anthony Goldrick (20)
Pat Kearney (50)
Anthony Coolican (23)
Martin Kearney (30)

By 9 p.m. the sea was calm again.

The following day, Saturday, 29 October 1927, the body of Anthony Kearney was recovered. On Sunday, 30 October, a coat identified as that worn by Thomas Lynott was carried ashore by the waves, as well as a muffler recognised as Pat Kearney's, and two fishermen's aprons. Later on that evening, nets were washed onto the strand. They contained some herring and dogfish.

None of the eight fishermen's bodies from the *Rose of Lacken* has ever been found, which was especially upsetting for the fishing families, who continue to live by the sea and look out each day to where their loved ones died.

Two sets of brothers died in the sinking. Pat Kearney was the skipper of the *Rose of Lacken*. He was married, though his wife and himself did not have any children. Thirty-year-old Martin Kearney, who died with him, was his brother. Twenty-two-year-old Michael and nineteen-year-old Pat Goldrick were also brothers.

The death of forty-year-old Thomas Goldrick was particularly sad. He had survived the First World War serving with the British navy in some of the toughest clashes at sea, including the Battle of Jutland. He was not a regular crew member of the *Rose of Lacken* but had gone fishing with them because they were short one man. So having survived battles at sea in a world war, he died in a gale, while fishing not far from the shore of his home place. Anthony Goldrick was a cousin of Thomas Goldrick. Fifty-year-old Thomas Lynott was the only man aboard who was a father. He had two children.

Newspaper reports of the time, carried in the local *Western People*, told how the crew of the *St Patrick* had cut away two nets they were fishing when the storm struck. One of the crew, Thomas Williams, said that all hope was abandoned when they were driven towards the rocks. 'We could make no headway and some of the oars were lost in the inky darkness. Then suddenly, the boat crashed against the rocks and the bottom of it was torn out. All of us, the whole crew of eight were thrown into the raging sea. I went down twice and when I came up the second time I caught hold of some floating wreckage. The next thing I found myself being swept onto the shore by a huge wave. This saved my life.'

The same wave swept the rest of the crew of the *St Patrick* ashore also, but Anthony Kearney was swept back out and he was never seen again. Other crews were also saved by the inexplicable actions of the sea, sparing some, taking others. In those times there were no rescue services to go to their aid, no lifeboats to call out, nor helicopters.

All of those who drowned were farmers and fishermen. They had small, uneconomic land holdings and had to fish to make a living. With no social welfare system at the time, families were left without their breadwinners and their plight was desperate. A public appeal was launched to assist them.

The paper's report included an interview with twenty-nine-year-old John McHale, described as 'the sturdy young skipper of the *Mystical Rose*,' who said: 'The wind was so strong that we could not even use our oars with any effect. We realised that we had no chance whatever of making it back to the pier, so with despair in our hearts, we tried to make for the strand in the hope that we might be washed ashore, for we could do little to help ourselves. Water came into the boat and we bailed it out as best we could. We were nearly mad with fear. Then the boat struck and it was on the strand and we managed to get ashore, where the people were screaming with fear for their sons or brothers or husbands who were still out on the water in that raging gale. It'll be many a long day before any fishing is done here again. The sea has frightened us.'

The fishing never did recover at Lacken, eighty-five-year-old James McLoughlin told me on Lacken Pier during the special eightieth anniversary commemoration ceremony at the new memorial:

'At my age there are things which I don't remember but even though I was only five at the time of the tragedy, that night and that time is written live on my memory and has always stayed there.' He was born in a house only a few yards from the strand where some of the boats were driven ashore and the Kearneys lived in the house next door. 'Some time during the night my mother came into the room where myself and my brother were asleep and she was crying and we knew something wasn't right. Then the front door opened and we could see Mrs Kearney come in and she was carrying a storm lamp and she was crying. More people came in. Men came carrying lamps and the priest came. My father came in carrying a bag on his shoulder with herring in it and they were all talking and Mrs Kearney asked him if he had seen her husband and he said he didn't but that some boats were in on the strand. Their boat had only made it after being driven back three times.'

In the stories that were told afterwards, some of the fishermen said that before the storm broke they saw an empty boat floating on the sea and that it might have been a warning to them. Fishermen are superstitious.

Some people left the area after the tragedy, to find work elsewhere and never again went fishing. They did not trust the sea any more and, as families left, the community around Lacken dwindled. But the villagers pledged never to forget the tragedy and that promise has been kept. At the rear of Lacken church there are stained glass windows which tell the story of the tragedy, underlining the promise which the local community had made that it would never be forgotten.

To be with the community at the special eightieth anniversary and the unveiling of the new memorial was to share a part of their story, to feel emotional with them as they remembered the devastation of their community in another October so many years ago. The stained glass windows were installed in 1997, twenty years after a stone memorial was erected on Lacken pier on the fiftieth anniversary of the drownings. The original memorial was rebuilt for the eightieth anniversary in local Lacken Stone as the permanent memorial. It includes a stone boat representing one of the vessels that went fishing that fateful night, *Rose of Lacken.*

Relatives of those who died took part in the mass at Lacken church, where I met Carol Whelan, granddaughter of Thomas Lynott, the only man with a family who had died in the tragedy, who was one of the main driving forces in organising the commemorative event.

'It is our hope that the men who lost their lives on 28 October in 1927 will never be forgotten,' she said. Lacken is a community which has never forgotten, a tribute to its sense of place in history.

Other areas of the Mayo coast were also hit by the storm which swept over the west coast of Ireland that night and so were areas of Galway. It is one of the worst disasters on record. It sprang up with surprising suddenness and without much warning, though later reports suggest that the barometer had fallen during the day, indicating an approaching change of weather. It was described as being of 'surprising violence, though of short duration'.

'It was among the poor and hardy fishermen of the Galway and Mayo coast that the heavy toll of life was exacted. In all, forty-five fishermen died in one night,' reported the papers. 'Caught in the sudden gale while fishing from small boats, they suffered heavily. Those who survived were the quickest to cut their nets adrift and make for the safety of the shore.'

As well as the nine at Lacken, nine fishermen died off Inishbofin; seventeen perished at Rossadelisk; Inniskea suffered the loss of ten and that island never recovered from the disaster.

Local stories tell of thousands of seals arriving into the area around Lacken Bay the morning after the tragedy, their squealing creating an eerie scene.

'It seemed like they were wailing for the dead,' one survivor said.

No more they'll laugh or row their boats to fish
    around the shore,
They're out upon the open sea, where the
    bounding billows roar;
They are gone but not forgotten, we're left to weep
    and mourn,
Lamenting for our missing ones, who never shall return.
T. McGinty

31

KINGDOM PORT

Fenit Port has a special place in my memory. It was there I saw my son leave on a voyage about which there was no certainty, and it was to there that I saw him return after a rough passage at sea. It was from there that I presented several editions of *Seascapes* and also reported several stories on television news. One of these I also filmed and that was before the days when reporters handled cameras and there was no such thing as VJs, video journalists.

The filming was because my cameraman had been landed – he said 'abandoned for a while' -because he was fairly seasick. So he had to be put off on Little Samphire Island, the small island off Fenit, on which the lighthouse stands. He was pretty glad to be ashore, on something solid, as we headed off again in a motorboat that dipped, dived, slammed and ploughed through the waves to cover a race in the West of Ireland sailing championships. But he was very glad when we got back, for he claimed the island was 'full of rats' and he had seen quite a few of them. Indeed, he seemed to have retreated as far as he could on the landing steps waiting and waving urgently to us, though we saw no sign of life other than his on the island.

Roy Hammond was my cameraman, my colleague and friend for many years, a great photographer and cameraman.

'Tommie, I am a sculptor in light,' he was fond of saying, but not where boats were concerned. He was a qualified pilot and being in the air was no problem – on a boat was not where he wanted to be. So when we would be assigned to a sailing or boating story – 'another wet story' by his description – or he would blame me for deciding to do one, there would be a fair bit of Roy's own ducking and diving in the wish that this particular cup would pass from him!

My son's journeys were on the *Jeanie Johnston*, on which he was second officer or second mate as it is called, on the original voyage to America. He brought her back on the return from Newfoundland, during which they encountered a Force 11, but the Kerry-built *Jeanie* rode it out like the fine vessel she was.

She left Fenit on Sunday, 16 February 2003, with a crowd estimated at over three thousand sending her off, along with a naval vessel salute. Former Tánaiste and Minister for Foreign Affairs, Dick Spring, sat in the guest enclosure overlooking the ship. 'I've been behind this project from day one,' he said. 'It was a tough road and there were a lot of battles along the way. I regret the Irish instincts that kick the dog when he's down but that's in the past now. The dream will be fulfilled.'

The leader of the Progressive Unionist Party of Northern Ireland, David Irvine, a strong supporter of the *Jeanie Johnston* project, was one of the special guests at Fenit: 'I saw *Jeanie* in Belfast and she attracted big crowds given that she was flying the tricolour, and given that she was wooden and wood burns well in Belfast. Twenty years ago she might have been burned but she wasn't and that tells us we're in changing times.'

After the speeches and blessings the band played the national anthem. The VIPs came ashore and the gangway was removed. Just before half past three the last line was released. The crowds cheered and waved as the band struck up *Anchors Aweigh*.

Fenit lifeboat, inshore rescue boats and a flotilla of other vessels added colour to the grey waters of the harbour as they escorted the *Jeanie Johnston* out into Tralee Bay on the first leg of her long-awaited voyage to North America. But she met heavy weather west of the Blaskets and many of the crew, including seasoned sailors, spent the first night reviewing previous meals. She took shelter in Valentia harbour, a prudent decision by Captain Tom McCarthy, who was in charge. He is a legend in his own lifetime in tall ships sailing and commanded *Asgard II* for many years. With six professional crew and the rest sail trainees, the right decision was to wait out the weather, but it caused me some moments of deep concern and almost led to a news story that would have caused panic amongst the parents of the trainees, another reason for which I remember Fenit – and Valentia.

The day after the *Jeanie* left, Monday, was a fine, sunny one in Cork where I live and the weather had moderated. But coming up to lunchtime, close to the one o'clock news bulletins on both radio and television, I received a call from the news desk to tell me that the *Jeanie* was sinking, a lifeboat had gone out to it and they had pictures showing it. A helicopter was also on the way – so 'get the story and get back to us quickly'. My first response was to close the door of the room I was using as a study!

Kathleen, my wife – and Rowan's mother of course (!) – was outside in the hallway, hoovering or cleaning, or something, and my first reaction, despite being a seasoned journalist, was concern over how she would react. I knew that she would be so worried that her son was aboard a sinking ship and waiting, hopefully, for rescue!

Then my reporter's instinct clicked back in – hang on a second: there were twenty-two on board; there was no helicopter which could lift that number together: it would be difficult for a lifeboat; and it was all happening off Valentia. Wasn't Seanie Murphy, a solid Kerryman, the coxswain of Valentia lifeboat, and wasn't he occasionally known to guide boats into the safety of the harbour in tough weather? Furthermore, didn't Tom McCarthy know that area of the coast and didn't he know Seanie?

But it was 12.40 p.m. and the news desk called again to say they were making it the main headline and what back-up support coverage would I need for television as well as radio.

'Hang on. Where did the news come from? Who told you the *Jeanie* is sinking?' I asked, at the same time as I was trying to dial the number I had for the *Jeanie* on my mobile phone by which I had arranged to keep in touch with them.

'We got the call from a guy on Valentia. He has photos and he's emailing them to us of the lifeboat going in to the rescue.'

The *Jeanie* phone wasn't answering: that voice which can sometimes be, and on this occasion was, infuriating, intoned the advice that it was either out of range or turned off. Not good, what next? A call to the coastguard. Had they heard anything about the *Jeanie*? Not a word. Was there a helicopter going to her? No.

Then a call to Valentia lifeboat. Seanie wasn't there, but the lifeboat was on the mooring in the harbour. Was the *Jeanie* there? Yes, anchored, sheltering. The weather wasn't good outside.

Thank God for that.

By now it was closing on 12.55 p.m. as I was reminded by the Sea Area Forecast from Met Éireann on the radio, warning of more rough weather to come. A quick, or if you want to take it, frantic, call to the news desk – kill that story, there was no problem with the *Jeanie*. She is safely sheltering.

So where did that story come from?

Someone, whom I have never identified, saw the lifeboat approaching the *Jeanie* as it struggled in the bad weather past the lighthouse on Valentia Island, and snapped off pictures. They then put two and two together and made five, telling the news desk that the *Jeanie* was sinking and the lifeboat was out. The lifeboat had actually gone out to give the *Jeanie* a guiding hand into the harbour. Lifeboats go on exercise frequently to keep their response levels high and she was also showing the friendship of the sea to Kerry's pride.

I remember how well Tralee Bay Sailing Club, perched atop the highest point overlooking Fenit Port, gave a send-off to the *Jeanie* and how marvellously they treated the crew they day the ship returned. It included several members of the club amongst the crew. The club laid on lunch and an evening meal for every one of the tired but happy crew. It was a welcome home of which Kerry could be proud.

On the quayside that afternoon when she docked, there was also a welcoming crowd. I noted that there were several politicians, including the man who had mouthed those awful words about the ship being burned in Brandon Bay. Now he wanted to be seen on television and in the newspapers welcoming her success. He did a rapid about face when I asked him how he felt about burning her now? He wasn't' seen on the pictures in my report!

I remember the words of Captain Tom McCarthy though, the man whom the crew praised for his leadership and his seamanship in that huge storm which hit them. They told me that he had come out of his cabin on the ship four hundred miles out from Ireland about an hour before the storm hit, telling his crew the ship wasn't happy and readying her for the approach of a storm. At that time the ship was, to quote one of the crew, 'barrelling along doing about twelve to fourteen knots and, we thought, going pretty well, eating up the distance to Ireland and home.'

Tom ordered the vessel brought about and readied for the storm. When it hit with ferocity, the ship was ready for it and, in the conditions, 'comparatively comfortable, so that we could even get a hot meal into us.' The crew told me that the ship talked to Tom and he understood her!

On Fenit quayside, when I congratulated him on the completion of the voyage, he said: 'Yes and no damage to her and no one lost. Now if even one person had gone overboard, the media would have ruined this ship and everyone associated with her, but she's a good ship and I had a good crew.'

It is said that Dick Spring was no handicap and probably a good help to Tralee Bay SC when they wanted to build the club in its spectacular location overlooking Brandon Bay. I met Dick one day at the club's boat park and, in his way – to which I had become accustomed over the years – he parried my question about his involvement by telling me that they had no problem in the club in accepting that Kerry would be better known for football than sailing, but sailing was on the way up and he was glad to help if he could.

It is one of the best-positioned clubs in the country and was there long before the new marina which has added considerably to the attraction of Fenit for sailing and boating. When the club was founded over half a century ago, they had to launch boats into the water with a manual crane. Things have changed a lot since than, as Paddy O'Sullivan, one of the founders, told me:

'When we first put forward the idea for a sailing club in Tralee Bay, there were those in the area whose first response was to tell us that the bay was too dangerous for sailing. "Commercial boats, they can manage in Tralee Bay, but pleasure craft will never survive," we were told.'

That was proved wrong and those who enjoy sailing in the bay can thank the determination of the founder members who met in the CYMS Hall in Tralee on 6 October 1956 to draw up a constitution for the new club and established its first committee, of which Paddy was the honorary secretary. The name chosen was Cumann Bad Traighli (Tralee Bay Sailing Club).

The members decided on the Heron dinghy as their first boat. Launching and retrieving these boats was none-too-easy. Slings were attached to a manual crane and they were lowered and recovered by winding them up and down with a manual handle. This facility was provided near the harbour office by the harbour master, T. F. Barrett, who had been elected the club's first commodore and who insisted that the handle be returned after every use. When, on occasions, that wasn't done, he locked away the handle to show members that the boats could not be launched without his assistance and that they needed to show a sense of responsibility and to learn it where it did not exist!

'It made for lively times around the use of the handle, but it was a good lesson in boat and harbour management,' said Paddy.

The club now has a membership of several hundred and a

fine club house, from which proud members will point out the club's own sailing school.

'It's in our own grounds and tell me what other club has its own sailing school?' I was asked, to which my answer was that I could not name one and that Kerry was leading the way in commitment to teaching the sport to young people, not only from the Kingdom county, but those outside who travel there for courses.

The sailing school building has been developed from a Nissen hut. There is no stopping the Kerry sailors. The school building has teaching classrooms, a drying room, offices, reception areas, wheelchair facilities, showers, changing rooms and can accommodate trainees. An average of three hundred a year were taking courses when I saw it.

The facilities have enabled them to stage major competitions, national and international, because cruiser racing and dinghies are all part of the mix in the club, which even bought kayaks to develop watersports and keep them going during the winter months.

Fenit is also a commercial port, the location where the Liebherr crane factory import and export. Huge crane parts lying adjacent to the port for shipping are a regular sight.

The original *Jeanie Johnston* carried emigrants from Tralee to Canada and it and others of the old sailing vessels would have used the channel midway between the Spa and Blennerville in Tralee Bay.

It is unusual for Kerrymen with their strong republican traditions to honour a link with a member of British royalty, but this part of the real 'kingdom' of Ireland is renowned for doing things its own way and, in these times, much has changed in relations with Britain. The connection with Britain's Prince of Wales came about as follows.

On the evening of 9 November 1930, the steamship *Co-operator* was reported to be in trouble in the channel. She had a crew of three – the captain, John Sullivan, Patrick Foley, who was the engine man, and Jerome Sullivan, the crewman. She had left Fenit at four o'clock in the afternoon and was not going far, carrying a cargo of corn for Tralee merchants in a time when transport by sea was more efficient for such a cargo. The routine voyage went normally until the boat reached a point opposite the Cockle Shell Road, midways between the Spa and Blennerville, when the weather worsened and storm conditions, which can be challenging in Tralee Bay, arose. A big wave washed over the deck. 'It was huge,' the crew later described it. 'It came out of nowhere.' Water cascaded down below into the engine room causing the boilers to explode as their water suddenly cooled down into clouds of steam. *Co-operator* listed quickly and began to sink. The corn, heavy with the water, expanded pressing against the vessel's sides.

The crew were left clinging to the mast, but fortunately their plight had been seen from shore. Three men, who had carried out rescues before in the bay, now rushed to the scene: John Cahill, his son Joseph, and Mr Nolan. They launched rowing boats and, battling tenaciously against the conditions, reached the distressed crew.

'We got there in time to get them off the mast and into the boats before they fell into the sea. The ship was drifting, blown along by the winds and it was difficult to manoeuvre, to get the men but we managed.'

The rescuers got the crew to shore at the Spa, but they were not in good condition. They were in a state of exhaustion, cold and shocked at the suddenness of what had happened. But, cared for by the local community, with hot drinks and warm clothes, they recovered and were taken by road to Tralee.

'News of what had happened had become known in the town and there was great relief when the three men were seen to be safe.'

The bay is shallow in areas and the *Co-operator* drifted into Frogmore where she grounded. Her cargo was badly damaged, but it was later reported that some of it was salvaged.

There was no lifeboat stationed in Fenit at that time. At the 107th annual meeting of the Royal National Lifeboat Institution in Central Hall, Westminster, London, bronze medals for their bravery were awarded by the Prince of Wales to the three men who had carried out the rescue. The Spa-Fenit Community Council marked the seventy-eighth anniversary of the rescue by unveiling a plaque recalling it.

'The suggestion was put forward and it was decided that this should be done, because the rescue is part of our maritime history in this community,' said Donal Crowley from the Community Council.

32

SLEEPING ON THE JOB AT THE BAILY LIGHTHOUSE AND HAUGHEY ON THE ROCKS IN BALTIMORE

Approaching Howth from Sutton along the coast road there is a right-hand turn to a private stretch of road that winds spectacularly above Dublin Bay, then bends and drops sharply to an impressive lighthouse. The first aeroplane to fly the Irish Sea narrowly missed this lighthouse and its pilot owed his rescue to the lighthousemen.

It is also the lighthouse where one of the staff decided to go to bed early and was asleep when a ship struck the cliff below his bedroom. Sixty passengers and crew aboard died, including the captain who, though dead, was later found guilty of culpable negligence!

The Baily was once the Commissioners of Irish Lights training centre for those entering the lighthouse service. And it was the last lighthouse on the Irish coast to be demanned and automated. Today it is a treasure house of memorabilia of the Irish Lighthouse service and to walk through it is to pass through history.

It is also a lighthouse where tragedy has occurred and beneath which many people have died, some probably because no action had been taken following the experience of a previous disaster that had involved the same Dublin shipping company!

It is one of Ireland's most important seamarks, located in a beautiful coastal setting, perched on a rocky promontory, a precipitous area accessed by steep steps and some uneven pathways, but magnificent to visit. It wasn't the first lighthouse on Howth Head; it had been preceded by a cottage-type lighthouse which was unique to Ireland when it was built with the permission of King Charles II and the light first exhibited there in 1667.

Above the Baily the battered walls of that cottage still remain. It used a coal-burning beacon on top of a square tower. The location, however, was not the best. It was so high up that the light was occasionally obscured by mist or cloud that would wrap around Howth Head and it was repositioned by the Corporation for Preserving and Improving the Port of Dublin. That organisation had taken over the then fourteen coastal lighthouses from the revenue commissioners in 1816. They had used the lighthouses to combat smuggling, as they provided observation platforms as well as a fairly basic safety system for shipping.

The new light was positioned further down the headland at the Little Baily, also known as Duncriffan, and, in an interesting historical note, this was the location where King Crimthan had his headquarters almost two thousand years previously.

I have never agreed a hundred per cent with the demanning of the lighthouses. I can understand the need for cost-cutting and the savings made by reducing staff, and that modern-day computerisation and electronics could do much of the work which staff did when the lighthouses were manned. But I have always believed, and still do, in the concept of 'eyes on the coastline', a watching service which would provide more security against drug-running and other illegal uses of our long coast. But that was not the job of the lighthouse service and, as with any other aspects of our maritime resources, the government ignored other possible uses of the lighthouses.

Yet it was the presence of a lighthouse which helped in the rescue of former Taoiseach Charles Haughey and his crew when his yacht, *Celtic Mist,* hit Mizen Head, in West Cork, in August 1986. Lightkeeper Richard Foran from Valentia Island was on duty and, with great courage, was lowered down the side of the Mizen to guide the Baltimore lifeboat to the rescue of the crew in their liferaft. Mizen Head Lighthouse is located on another rocky promontory at the south-western tip of Ireland and reached by a bridge across a gorge. To walk around it is to appreciate the drop to the sea and the courage which Richard Foran showed that night.

I remember meeting the late Mr Haughey in Bushe's pub in Baltimore the morning after the rescue. Bushe's is a traditional landmark for the boating fraternity and there were many of them there, together with the waiting media corps, of which I was one, when Charles Haughey came in to tell his story. Before he did that, a round of drinks was ordered for everyone, a mixed concoction of liquid, served with plenty of ice and which was promptly named 'Haughey on the Rocks'.

As I remember that day, Mr Haughey was effusive in his praise of the lightkeepers and the lighthouse service and pledged that he would not allow lighthouses to be demanned, which was the threat the staff faced at the time. He never delivered on that promise, probably didn't have the power to do so because the Commissioners of Irish Lights are independent of government and, unless the state was prepared to take over the service, which it wasn't, the lighthouses were going to be demanned – and so they were.

I raised with Mr Haughey that promise in later times, but nothing was ever resolved. He was a man with a great commitment to the sea and though he did quite a bit to promote the marine sphere, like many others of the Irish political class, he gave undertakings that were not realised.

The Mizen is linked to the Baily by some of the artefacts stored in the Lighthouse Museum and also by the unusual and difficult location in which it was built, but the Baily was in existence before the Mizen. As I arrived at the Baily, negotiating the narrow road close to the lighthouse and parked my car, I marvelled at how the builders of so long ago had managed, with facilities that, compared with today's construction resources, must have been quite basic.

The first light was displayed at the Baily on 17 March 1814 – appropriately a new safety mark on the Irish coastline on the national saint's feast day. But that association with holiness did not guarantee any spiritual or magical protection for shipping and several vessels struck the rocks close to the Baily, despite the warning light.

After the City of Dublin Steam Packet Company's paddle steamer, *Prince*, hit the cliffs near the 'Nose of Howth', as the area is called, in thick fog on 3 August 1846, there was a lot of discussion about whether a sound signal from the lighthouse would have helped avoid the collision. The board of the corporation concluded that it 'could not be certain' that if there had been a fog bell at the lighthouse, the accident would have been prevented, but agreed that it 'would be advisable' to erect a fog bell which would be operated by machinery in the lighthouse.

But that was not done and seven years later, another City of Dublin Steam Packet company paddle steamer, the *Queen Victoria*, ran onto the Casana Rock between the 'Nose' and the Baily in a snowstorm on 15 February 1853. That was a ship that did not want to let go the grip which it had onto the land, but it was also a ship on which there was heavy loss of life.

The ship had been built in 1837 as a 337-ton paddle steamer. She left Liverpool on St Valentine's Day, 14 February 1853, with 112 passengers and crew aboard and a general cargo. At 2 a.m. the following morning, in a snowstorm she struck the cliffs close to the Baily.

Eight of the passengers managed to jump ashore, making their way up the cliff to the lighthouse, even while the captain of the *Queen Victoria* was trying to reverse it back off the rocks. To his relief and that of everyone else on board, he succeeded and the ship slid back into the water. But the relief didn't last long. It had sustained a lot of damage and began to fill with water. It drifted back towards the Baily and again struck the rocks, this time almost directly below the lighthouse and sank. However, it did not disappear from sight – the bowsprit still touched the shore and remained clinging to it for some time afterwards. A lifeboat was launched, but capsized and sank. Those aboard it were drowned.

Another City of Dublin Steam Packet Company vessel, the paddle steamer *Roscommon*, got to the scene and rescued between forty and fifty, the only other survivors from the tragedy, apart from those who jumped ship and made their way to the lighthouse. All the others aboard were drowned, including the captain.

Subsequently, there was a protracted trial in which the jury found that the captain and the mate were guilty of culpable negligence in failing to reduce speed during the snowstorm, which had obscured the lights of the lighthouse. The corporation conducted its own inquiry and found that the light on the Baily was in perfect working order, but that when the *Queen Victoria* struck the cliff below the lighthouse, the assistant keeper who should have been on watch had retired to bed early! He was dismissed from the service. What about the sound signal that would surely have helped alert the ship to the rocks? Its installation had been agreed as 'advisable' seven years before, following the other Dublin Steam Packet Company paddle steamer, the *Prince*, striking the rocks. That fog bell should have been erected in 1847, but had been postponed 'due to the urgency of other works being undertaken around the coast'.

Two months after the *Queen Victoria* tragedy, the Corporation for Preserving and Improving the Port of Dublin informed the Board of Trade that the fog bell was 'in the course of erection'. It was in operation by the end of April 1853, but there is no record of anyone in authority having suffered any penalties for its non-installation over the previous six years.

The only person to suffer was the assistant lightkeeper, who took an early night. No one in management was held responsible. Some things were not much different then to what they are now!

Walking through the lighthouse, it is surprising to come upon a big model of a very old aeroplane, the type that makes one wonder how they managed to fly at all and what kept them up in the air. This was the plane in which the first ever successful crossing of the Irish Sea was made. Captain Owen Deignan, who was then consultant curator and who previously served as inspector of lights and marine superintendent with Irish lights, told me the story.

Although the name Baily is often heard on the radio and television, the lighthouse is not open to the public due to its precarious location. The project manager of the lighthouse museum is Captain Kieran O'Higgins, deputy inspector in the marine department of Irish Lights. However, Irish Lights will help when possible with visits if requests are made to them.

33

THE *LOCH RYAN* – A WEST CORK SCHOONER – ATTACKED BY THE GERMAN AIR FORCE, A FAMILY RUINED AND THE SHAMEFUL ATTITUDE OF TWO GOVERNMENTS

One of the most extraordinary stories I came across on *Seascapes* is that of the *Loch Ryan*, an Irish schooner attacked without warning and with clearly murderous intent, by the Luftwaffe, the German Air Force, early in the Second World War, in clear violation of the rules of international law regarding the treatment of neutrals. It is a story of cover-up by the Irish government, an apparent misleading of the Dáil by the Taoiseach of the time, the banning of newspapers from mentioning the story, and the financial ruining of a family who battled for sixty years without success to get an apology and compensation from the German government. It remains still the only war time reparation claim from Ireland that has not been resolved by the Germans. Sadly, the man who brought the story to me died while he still fought a lengthy battle to gain that apology.

The *Loch Ryan* was a Skibbereen-registered schooner which traded to Britain. On 15 August 1940, she sailed from Par in Cornwall for Arklow with a cargo of china clay aboard. This was a vital commodity for Irish production needs as war began and

Youghal strand.

Ballyquin Beach, Ardmore, Co. Waterford.

The Hook Peninsula stretches out into the Celtic Sea and provides beautiful vistas, pretty villages and an impressive lighthouse to visitors.

Youghal Sunrise.

Old fishing boat at Kenmare, Co. Kerry.

Kilmore Quay Memorial: The sea affects all irish people

Waves crashing, Dingle, Co. Kerry.

The interlocking basalt columns of the Giant's Causeway, Co. Antrim.

Clogher Strand, Co. Kerry.

Fishing is essential to Irish coastal regions.

Fishing at Inch Beach, Co. Kerry.

was classed as 'essential raw material'. She was commanded and owned by Captain James Nolan, who obeyed British Admiralty instructions by keeping his vessel 'off the Dodman, four miles off the Lizard and four miles off the Longships Lighthouse'.

She passed the Longships later that night and altered course for Ireland. The following afternoon at 14.10, three German planes attacked her, though she was flying the Irish tricolour from her stern. For Captain Nolan from North Street in Skibbereen, his chief engineer, Jerome McCarthy from Baltimore, and mate, John Hegarty from Skibbereen, it was a terrifying ordeal. It lasted for forty-five minutes during which, according to the crew, the planes made twelve machine gun attacks and then dropped six bombs at the vessel. Captain Nolan thought 'this was the finish of us', and the Germans, apparently thinking the same, flew off, leaving the crew to their fate.

Luckily, the stoutly-built *Loch Ryan* stayed afloat and the crew managed to turn the vessel and limped towards Mount's Bay. The *Western Morning News* newspaper reported that it was a miracle that the vessel remained afloat:

'The vessel was a miracle afloat when it arrived in Mount's Bay. Practically all her rigging had been cut away by machine-gun bullets. Her masts were chipped in scores of places by bullets and there were hundreds of holes in her sails. But the crew were amazing, just like their ship. During the attack they took cover under the poop deck. It is the skipper's opinion that the cargo of china stone saved the ship.

'"We were about forty miles from the coast at two o'clock on Friday when the three German planes flew over and started to attack us," he said. "They were flying in line ahead and went over us one after the other, just above our masts. They were at us for three-quarters of an hour and we were machine-gunned four times by each plane. For a time we stayed in the wheelhouse but then things got too hot and we took cover under the poop deck where there was an iron deck and two inches of planking above our heads. The planes dropped two bombs each. Four went into the sea, but two came right aboard, one fell through the forward deckhouse, went through the deck and burst down below. The other one went through the hatch and exploded in the hold. When a bomb burst inside the hull I thought the ship was going to open out, I thought we were finished. When the German planes flew off I thought the ship could not survive and, with the lifeboat destroyed, we thought we would try to make a raft, but then I found that she was still bearing up and there was no water coming in, so we stayed aboard," said Captain Nolan.

'He was talking to our reporter in a cabin where the floor was covered with splinters of glass, the bunks were littered with it and shards of timber and items had been blown off the cabin walls. Captain Nolan said he thought it was the cargo of china stone that was solid enough to prevent a bomb going through the bottom of the ship and strong enough to absorb the shock of an explosion. The Captain's main concern was to get his ship repaired and get back to sea. But showing the strength of these Irish seamen, they were far from finished, though shocked by the attack. In fact a piece of bacon was frying with a tempting smell in the galley as our reporter talked to the skipper and the crew went about their duties, even though the galley area was buckled and bulged in all shapes.'

The *Loch Ryan* was escorted to Falmouth where repairs were made costing £1,680, a lot of money at the time, and she was able to sail to Arklow on 21 October of that year.

The bombing was extensively reported in British newspapers, national and regional, but the Irish government suppressed immediate news of the attack through the direct intervention of the Censorship Board. One Irish regional paper which did report the incident was severely reprimanded and threatened by the authorities. It was over a week after the attack before a report appeared in *The Irish Press*, the paper regarded as closest to the government. Why this was done is not clear, because in 1940 and 1941 there were several German attacks on shipping in the Irish Sea and coastal areas and they were reported, but reporting of the attack on the *Loch Ryan* was prevented. The Nolan family believed that this may have been, to quote Denis Nolan, son of the *Loch Ryan*'s captain, 'partly due to the apparent policy of the Irish Free State government of the day to avoid any disagreement with Germany even if it meant abandoning one small part of the unprotected Irish merchant fleet.'

Captain Nolan's problems were not over. When the *Loch Ryan* arrived in Arklow she was subjected to a Warrant of Arrest, taken out in the Irish Admiralty Court (High Court) by the British insurance company, the Mutual War Risk Insurance Association because of a dispute over the insurance and repair costs.

Soon after the attack, Captain James Nolan instructed solicitors to take the matter up with the Irish government with a view to obtaining immediate compensation from the Germans. Possibly because the incident was one of the first involving German air attacks on Irish property, the response of the government was initially cautious, and then became less supportive. It ignored a crucial fact, that the *Loch Ryan* was attacked in international waters, *the day before the Germans declared a blockade in the area* and warned that they would attack shipping found there.

Denis Nolan, Captain Nolan's son, was the man who brought the story to me:

'My father had to sell the ship to resolve the issue and that ended 160 years of seafaring in our family. We lost the complete family seafaring/trading business in which we had been involved since the early part of the nineteenth century. My father suffered humiliation and hardship during the 1940s and 1950s as a result and so did his family, because we had lost our business and there was no income. During these years my father had to return to sea as a member of a crew when he was aged sixty-one and to go on serving at sea until he was seventy-three to provide for his young family.'

As he told me the story, it was clear how upset and angry he felt and the disillusion he had with the Irish government which, he believed, had not honoured his father, nor defended the seafaring traditions and rights of Irish sailors.

The Department of External Affairs, after the incident had been reported by Captain Nolan to the Irish authorities, directed the Irish embassy in Berlin, with whom Ireland maintained relations as a neutral nation, to protest. The initial response was that the attack had occurred in an area declared by the Germans to be a 'blockade zone'. Accordingly, the German authorities would take no responsibility for the fate of any vessel in the area. But the attack had actually taken place *the day before the Germans declared a blockade zone,* so they were guilty of unlawfully attacking a neutral vessel in what were then international waters. This was a criminal action

The Department of External Affairs in Dublin said that it was only later realised that the attack had actually taken place the day before that blockade zone was declared by the Germans.

Realising this, the Irish embassy in Berlin said it made a fresh approach on that basis and was again rebuffed, this time being told that the Germans had no record of the attack and could not, therefore, take responsibility. After that, it appears that the department decided that no further progress on the issue was likely to be made until after the war.

But on 5 February 1941 the matter was raised through a parliamentary question in the Dáil. The Taoiseach, Eamon de Valera, who was also Minister for External Affairs, responded to Deputy O'Neill, who asked for a statement about the attack, about protests to the German government and if the Irish government would make any provision for payment of compensation to Irish vessels that might meet the same fate as the *Loch Ryan*.

The Taoiseach said:

'My information, which is based on a statement by the master of the vessel, is that the attack on the *Loch Ryan* took place not off the Irish coast, but at a point forty miles north-west by north of Land's End in Cornwall. The matter was taken up with the German government and in December a reply was received to the effect that, as the *Loch Ryan* was not in Irish territorial waters but in the blockade area and as no guarantees had been given to any country as regards shipping in this area, the German government could not accept responsibility. With regard to insurance, that is a matter for the owner. It would appear that in the case the precautions taken by the owner in regard to insurance were not adequate.'

This statement did not declare to the Dáil the most salient point, that the attack took place the day before that blockade zone was declared by the Germans. The government knew this and had made a repeated protest on this issue, but the fact that it was ignored in his official Dáil reply by the Taoiseach appeared to indicate that the Irish government did not want to pursue the issue with the Germans, for whatever reason.

'My father was shocked and dismayed by the extraordinary posture of the Taoiseach in the Dáil,' Denis Nolan told me. 'The Taoiseach acknowledged that the attack took place in what was described as the blockade area when he knew full well that it did not. The Taoiseach was all but validating the German view that they could not be held responsible for the attack. My father felt this was a betrayal by the Taoiseach who wanted to dismiss the compensation claim as quickly as possible so that it would not embarrass him with the Germans. This vital flaw misled the Dáil and was not corrected for several months, when it was eventually pointed out to the Germans that they were wrong, but valuable time had been wasted and the Germans were able to respond that their air squadrons were dispersed throughout France at this stage and they could not trace a record of the incident. The Irish government did not press or pursue the case but cynically consigned the *Loch Ryan*, my father, his crew and our families to a political limbo in keeping with their political policy of the time, not to annoy the Germans.'

This was how the Dáil debate went:

The Taoiseach was questioned by James Dillon: Arising out of the reply, do we admit the right of foreign governments to open fire upon our ships and our nationals and does our failure to make any rejoinder to that reply by the government of the German Reich imply our consent to the outrageous proposal that the German government or any other government can open fire on peaceful merchant ships and destroy them on the high seas?

Taoiseach: My statement does not imply anything. I have given the facts.

Mr Dillon: No, but I am asking, does the failure to make any rejoinder to the German government's refusal to accept liability for this murderous attack on a ship on the high seas imply that our government thinks no protest is proper against attack upon a peaceful Irish merchant ship and its crew, sailing the high seas, by the armed forces of the German government?

Taoiseach: There were no implications in my reply. I have stated the facts.

Mr Dillon: Does the Minister assert the right of our mercantile marine to sail the high seas unhindered by murderous attacks of this kind?

Taoiseach: Yes, but other neutral states have not been able to get their views accepted either.

Mr Dillon: But we assert that view?

Taoiseach: Yes, we assert all that we are able to assert.

Mr O'Neill: Perhaps I might be permitted to put a supplementary to my own question? The last part of the question raises the matter of the general provision of compensation in such cases. Can the Minister add anything to that?

Taoiseach: I have nothing to add to the statement I have given.

Mr O'Neill: Am I right in saying that this is a matter which is under investigation and that it will be considered?

Taoiseach: The whole question with regard to shipping has been fully considered.

That was the last action which the Irish government took during the war years in defence of the innocent seafarers and their ship which had been attacked without warning. It did not indicate a government which had much concern for seafarers. A lot of correspondence followed, but there were no further recorded approaches to the Germans, though it seems that on one subsequent occasion the Irish embassy then in Bonn, was asked to raise the case, but there is no record of any action in the department's files.

'My father's dignity and integrity were such that he would not exploit the incident, or take political advantage or seek publicity that would have been to his advantage. He was not a man like that, so despite his personal anger and upset, the issue was pushed aside and it was 1953 before our family was told anything and then it was that we would have to wait for treaties to be signed and that was still the case when we heard more in 1960. It was eventually 1990, after both my father and mother, Anne, had died that the family heard more. Throughout all that time we received no news, no status report, not even one message of support from any Irish government, despite the fact that many of the Irish victims of various German attacks on land and sea had been compensated for decades earlier by the Irish or German governments.'

Captain James Nolan, born in 1880, was sixty years old when his ship was attacked. He had been at sea since the age of sixteen, following his family's seagoing tradition, established since the early part of the nineteenth century. He had first sailed on his father's schooner. Later on, he broadened his experience for many years on large ocean-going vessels before he returned to Ireland to take over the family's shipping and trading business. Amongst the ships he sailed on as master were the *Jessie* and the *Pricilla*, both schooners owned by the Nolan family, carrying general cargo between Belgium, Holland, France, the Mediterranean,

Britain and Ireland. As a young master he sailed to the Sea of Azov in 1913.

From the time of her purchase in 1927, the *Loch Ryan* traded between Britain, France, Belgium and Ireland, although from the early 1930s the business was generally between English, Welsh and Irish ports. She had previously been called the *Vlaardingen* and the *Catharina*. She was an auxiliary schooner, 111 feet long and had been built in 1913 in Hoogesand in Holland.

The attack on the *Loch Ryan* had a devastating effect on the Nolan business, on Captain Nolan's career, his health and his family. He suffered from recurring nightmares for a considerable time after the ordeal of being bombed and straffed aboard his small, defenceless schooner. He did not have sufficient money to pay for the shortfall between what was available from insurance for the schooner and the cost of the repairs and related expenses. He tried but failed to obtain finance. There were no loans or guarantees of support to help his business continue. With a family of six to support he tried desperately to avoid the seizure and sale of his major asset, the *Loch Ryan*. But his 200-ton schooner, the last of the active auxiliary schooners of what was then a small Irish coastal fleet was seized on the demands of the British insurance company.

Although the *Loch Ryan* had a good record and was respected for trading on the British coastline and the crew had been praised for how they had reacted to being attacked, Captain Nolan suspected that British anger at Irish neutrality and perceived lack of support for the British war effort was reflected by the British insurance company in its stance that the ship had been repaired in a British facility and he should make good the balance between the cost of the repairs and the value for which the ship was insured. No one had expected that it would be murderously attacked by a belligerent warring force. Bereft of financial support, with the British insurance company demanding its money, there was a forced sale of the *Loch Ryan*, which was concluded at a 'distress' price.

Denis Nolan approached me about the story after the sixtieth anniversary of the sinking had passed without any advance of the family's case. He made it clear that the Nolans still did not accept that the Irish government could not achieve a just settlement on behalf of the family. 'The Taoiseach misled the Dáil when the attack was debated in 1941, repeating the German assertion that the incident took place in the blockade zone when he knew full well that it did not. He said he had given the facts, and his refusal to contradict the German statement, which he knew to be untrue, was a critical factor in the subsequent mismanagement of the claim by the Irish government. Our family continues to contend that the attack on our unarmed ship took place outside the blockade zone and was an attack on Irish property and should have been settled along with the other incidents for which Irish citizens were compensated. We feel betrayed by our own government whom we hold fully responsible both for the original suppression of the truth and subsequent mismanagement of the case. Our case is a just one and there should be an apology from the German government and our own government to us.'

Investigating this case I came across a note from the Department of Foreign Affairs to the Irish embassy in Bonn in June 1994. Demonstrating again the unwillingness of the government and its diplomatic arm to create too much fuss about the *Loch Ryan*, the author of the letter said:

'My over-riding concern is that the Department of the Marine [which had also been approach by the Nolans] may expect us to make a publicly visible fuss over this case, regardless of whether it actually yields tangible results.'

Amongst the documents which came into my possession was a letter drafted by the Legal Division of the Department of Foreign Affairs, dated 7 December 1999, but seemingly never issued, intended to be sent to the German government and which referred to 'unlawful German actions during the war ... It is submitted that full and adequate compensation is justified as directly serving to ameliorate a financial loss that specifically and uniquely affected the Nolan family in its entirety and which that family has had to bear fully, along with the consequences which have flown from it, for the past half-century and more.' It is not clear why this letter, seeking compensation from Germany for the Nolan family, was never issued.

In August 2000, Denis Nolan again wrote to the Department of Foreign Affairs, conveying the unanimous feeling of the surviving members of the Nolan family:

'We consider an acknowledgement of responsibility by the German government to be very important. We also feel that a full apology to the Nolan family from the appropriate authority or authorities is long overdue. While we have not yet been officially invited by either the German or Irish governments to specify an acceptable compensation amount that is due to us, we shall do so if officially requested. There should be no misunderstanding about the issue. We seek the substantial compensation that is due to us for the loss suffered over sixty years by our family from the complete loss of the family seafaring/trading business in which we had been involved since the early part of the nineteenth century.'

At the time, West Cork Deputy Jim O'Keeffe of Fine Gael also took up the issue on behalf of the family, but sensed that there was no strong commitment at government level, apart from the practised diplomatic approach of correspondence, which was not likely to achieve a resolution satisfactory to the Nolans. In May 2001 the Department of Foreign Affairs wrote to Denis Nolan, outlining how the German government was avoiding responsibility for any compensation. The department put the damage caused to the ship at £1,301-17-5p 'which is equivalent to some £45,600 – €57,900 in present-day values.' The letter said that 'the Irish authorities consider that there is a case for compensation by the German authorities to the family of the vessel's owner and that accordingly the issue warranted further consideration by Germany.'

But the German government refused to give any consideration to reparation claims more than fifty years after the end of the war, even though the Nolan family had been pursuing it since it happened and had the evidence to show that German planes attacked an Irish vessel in international waters, where no blockade had been declared on the day the attack took place.

'Germany is not willing to re-open a sixty-year-old claim now,' wrote the department, saying that it 'very much regretted that it has not been possible to achieve a satisfactory outcome.'

This was the third time within the past six years that the case had been raised with the German authorities and on each occasion there was a negative response.

'There is no evidence of a disposition to change in the German position and, in light of this, the prospect of an admission of responsibility by Germany at a future time must be considered unlikely. Moreover, there is no international legal forum before which Germany can be compelled to appear in this case. For these reasons, further pursuit of the claim with the authorities in Berlin does not hold out the prospect of achieving a positive result,' said the department.

In June 2001 the newspapers reported that the then Minister for Foreign Affairs, Brian Cowen, had said the government had 'given up hope' of winning compensation for the Nolan family. He said it was unlikely, following a meeting between German officials and the Irish ambassador in Berlin, that the German government would ever pay compensation for the outstanding Irish reparation claim from the Second World War.

After his schooner was bombed, Captain James Nolan never again sailed as master of his own ship, never again commanded the income to adequately maintain his large family, the oldest of whom was only fifteen. The resulting collapse in the family's social status from comparative prosperity to deprivation caused considerable anguish and imposed a strain on Mrs Anne Nolan, who had herself a history of anxiety from an earlier sea tragedy. As a girl of thirteen she was saved in dramatic circumstances when the vessel *Thomas Joseph* foundered and sank near Sherkin Island, amongst Carbery's Hundred Isles in West Cork in 1919. Amongst those who died was her fifteen-year-old-sister. As the repercussions of the *Loch Ryan* impacted on her family, with economic and financial deprivation, her earlier traumas of nightmares and worry returned to upset her. Added to this, Captain Nolan had to return to sea, the business he knew, but this time in the lower ranks of seaman, to earn a living.

It is ironic that amongst the vessels he served on was the Irish Shipping's *M.V. Kerlogue*, a small trading vessel which saved the lives of 160 German seamen in the Bay of Biscay in December

1943. They were the survivors from the German destroyer, *T26*, which had been sunk in a battle. The *Kerlogue* on her way to Ireland was buzzed by a German plane, flashing lights to get the ship to follow it to where the German sailors were found, rescued and carried to Cobh. One can only imagine how James Nolan felt as the German plane came over the Irish vessel.

Captain James Nolan died in 1962. His son, Denis Nolan, continued the campaign for apology, compensation and recognition of the attack on the *Loch Ryan* for many years, but died recently while still battling the family's case with the Irish and German governments.

'Whatever political justification there may have been for the Irish government policy of the day, there can be no excuse for the cynical manner in which successive Irish governments repeatedly ignored requests for fair consideration of our case,' he told me during my investigation of the story for one of our *Seascapes* programmes. 'The victims of other German acts of aggression on Irish shipping and property were compensated by either the Irish or German governments. We are an Irish family whose business was destroyed by the German Air Force and shamefully betrayed and abandoned by the government of the Irish Free State.'

The *Loch Ryan* affair remains unresolved, the only outstanding Irish war reparation claim still rejected by the German government.

34

THE SAILOR OF SLIGO

Rosses Point would be better known for golf, but there is also a bar in that area named after the America's Cup, a legendary sailing event. Approaching Sligo City from the north, you need to make a right-hand turn before entering the city – or, if coming the other way, turn to port, that's left – and head towards the sea to find a lovely yacht club building. Here there is a unique sailor, a man who at seventy-three still races in fourteen-foot dinghies and sees no reason why he should give it up.

Gus Henry is one of the outstanding figures in Irish sailing. He led the revival of Sligo Yacht Club, which had originally been founded in 1821 but had not been active for over sixty years. Honoured as 'Volunteer of the Year' by the Irish Sailing Association for fifty years of service to the sport, he has kept sailing going at Rosses Point.

I met Gus one evening at the club when he was preparing to run the World GP14 Dinghy Racing Championships as race officer, a demanding role, but one for which he was well prepared. Gus was the first commodore and was re-elected several times as he led the club in developing the sport.

'I suppose I foolishly stood still a few times and got hit with the job!'

The original Sligo Yacht Club did most of its racing on Lough Gill. Records show that the club had not been active long before it was completely disbanded in the 1920s. However, Sligo has an excellent maritime history and there were several sailing craft on Lough Gill and Sligo Bay where Gus Henry sailed.

Gus Henry has been the mainstay of Sligo Yacht Club right from when he and five Sligo sailors decided to reform on Lough Gill the club that had become inactive since the 1920s.

'When we started we built six GP14 dinghies and three other people purchased these boats, so we had nine GP14s. So we decided to start a club in Sligo with a membership of nine.'

From these small beginnings, Gus has led the development of Sligo Yacht Club to its present strength, with around two hundred members. It has the largest GP14 fleet in Ireland and the British Isles, a strong vibrant Mirror fleet and an enviable record of hosting events for many classes at all levels up to and including world championships.

The GP14 is the foundation of the club's success and, as well as sailing and racing the boats, Gus Henry has built them.

'Getting young people to take up sailing is important for the continued growth of the sport and the club,' says Gus, who has shown a keen interest in promoting the Mirror Class. He encourages young people to take up sailing and has supported and helped train them to represent the club successfully on the national scene.

A decision was made to build a clubhouse in the early 1970s. This was a big challenge for the membership as sailing was not hugely popular in Sligo. The cost of membership was only £3 a year, but the members agreed that they would have to get a clubhouse.

'We reckoned that we would never make much of sailing in the area if we did not have the facilities and we took upon ourselves the spending of £32,000 which, in real terms, was quite a lot of money then. In fact it was enormous. But I reckoned it had to be done. There had been other attempts to develop sailing in Sligo but they had not succeeded. The provision of a clubhouse would help us, so the project started. My father had been involved in previous attempts to develop sailing but they had never succeeded in getting a lot of success; a base was needed and so we took the leap of getting premises.'

The clubhouse was gradually extended and in 1987 something special was added – the America's Cup Bar. These premises actually lasted until 2006 when they were developed into a new purpose-built facility. As commodore, Gus was the driving force to set up the project and a team to lead it. This time it cost a lot more than the £32,000 spent on the original building, many times more. Close on €1.5 million, which the club members undertook to cover when financial arrangements were made. It was another challenge for the members, but there was strong support, underlining the commitment to sailing in Sligo, and it was built in time for the GP14 Dinghy World Championships.

That event at Sligo Yacht Club yielded a lot of money for the local tourist economy and had been awarded to Sligo because the club had built up the biggest GP14 fleet of any single club in Ireland or Britain. There are forty of them. This is a lot of a one-design class, meaning all the boats are the same, which makes for even racing, since the deciding factor is the skill of the crew and their sailing ability, the truest form of race sailing. In weekly club racing nights, between thirty and forty boats take part.

Gus came around the side of the clubhouse to meet me, heading for the dinghy park where the boats were kept.

'I saw you with a rudder under your arm. Are you still sailing in dinghies?'

'Yeah, I still race, I even won last night,' he replied. 'I think the others might have allowed me to win, just for my age and that they knew you were coming to interview me tonight, as a boost to my morale.'

He had won, but not because anybody wanted to let him past them. Gus is still a doughty competitor.

'You haven't lost your enthusiasm for sailing?'

'No, I think maybe I have got more foolish as the years passed!'

'What keeps you going in the sport?'

'I love sailing. There is a great challenge to it and an enjoyment and I'll keep going just as long as I can get into the boat and sail it.'

Sligo Yacht Club and Irish sailing owe this tireless worker a huge thank-you for all his voluntary contributions for the benefit of the sport.

Rosses Point provides good sailing grounds. As you drive towards the club, cruisers are anchored close to the clubhouse in a sheltered inlet, while the dinghies have their own boat park to the west of the club with slipways for launching – a short sail and a move 'around the corner and we are in decent racing water'. The location also provides what many other clubs cannot, in that the craft are easily watched from the shore, either from the clubhouse balcony or the waterfront. There is a tidal rise and fall of four metres in the waters off Rosses Point, which can present quite a challenge for the dinghies, but does make their crews into good sailors.

Sligo Yacht Club hosted the Enterprise World Championships in 1979. In 1977 and again in 1980, the Scorpion Class held their European Championship in Sligo. The IDRA 14 Dinghy Class National Championships were hosted by Sligo in 1976, 1978, 1982 and 1983. The club also hosted two very successful Dinghy Weeks in 1978 and again in 1983. Mirror Week, incorporating Junior and Senior National Championships, was first hosted by Sligo in 1974, ten years later in 1984, in 1999 and again in 2003. In 1987, the Mirror World Championships took place in Sligo. In 2008, the Mirror European Championships will be held in Sligo. In 1998, Sligo Yacht Club welcomed visitors from all over the country to Rosses Point for the GP14 National Championships and in 2000 the Mermaid Nationals. The GP14 Class again came to Rosses Point for their Irish National Championships in 2005 as a prelude to the World championships in 2006.

35

FRIGHTENED AND UNCERTAIN
ON THE ATLANTIC

Stepping aboard *NCB Ireland* as she lay alongside Pier 66 in the Florida sunshine was a move into the unknown. I had a fair deal of experience, so I thought, as a sailor in dinghy and cruiser racing around the south of Ireland. I had raced one of the world's toughest offshore races, the Round Ireland, several times; I'd taken part in a Round Ireland and Britain Race; raced from Ireland to Scotland; around Scotland and back again to Northern Ireland. But crossing the Atlantic was a challenge of another kind altogether.

NCB Ireland, the first-ever Irish entry in a world sailing event, had been setting headlines since it set off in what was then known as the Whitbread Round the World Race, now the 'Volvo Race', but for all the wrong reasons. She had not been anywhere near the top of the fleet, was in fact rather low, and despite all the hype about her, she had not realised the initial hopes for her.

Four million pounds was a huge Irish investment for the 1989-1990 race. Dermot Desmond's NCB Group led the business backing, then came Aer Lingus, ESB International, Jameson Whiskey (Irish Distillers) and Irish Life. The Insurance

Corporation of Ireland, the Jefferson Smurfit Group, weighed in and there was support from many others. As Taoiseach, Charles Haughey was also a supporter of the project and, if his name crops up again in maritime affairs, it is simply because over the years he is the only politician who has shown any concern or interest. There may be some who do not like that, but the facts are always sacred where I as a journalist am concerned.

At the time Dermot Desmond was investing in moves to make Ireland an international financial centre and the Sail Ireland project was intended to promote Ireland internationally through the Round the World Race. It was the subject of massive international publicity, and benefited from his support in the region of £1.4 million. That was Irish pounds, a time when 'money was real money!'

Howard Kilroy, another successful businessman, joined in support, along with others who had lot of financial and management skills, such as Paddy Moriarty, Des Burke-Kennedy, Fergal Quinn, Robert Dix, a later president of the Irish Sailing Association. I met, talked to and interviewed all of them as I reported this evolving story for *Seascapes* and radio and television news. Other names associated with the project were the late Hugh Coveney, who for a short time was Minister for the Marine. He had great potential, but did not have time to demonstrate it because he lost his ministerial post in a political difficulty which would be very minor compared with what has occurred in recent times. There was also Bernie Cahill, Clayton Love Jr, John Gore-Grimes, Harold Cudmore, Tom Power, John Bourke and many others.

I remember the start from the Solent, one of the world's great sailing locations and the heart of English sailing, on 2 September

1989. I was commentating on it from broadcast cabins which had been set up on the foreshore at Cowes and what a sight it was. There were four and a half thousand craft of all kinds on the water to see the start by twenty-three yachts representing several nations from all around the world. There seemed to be every type of craft. There were canoes, kayaks, small boats with outboard motors, yachts, motorboats of all kinds and even a paddle-steamer. Almost suicidal drivers of fast boats zipped in and out amongst the fleet, and sometimes boats seemed far too close to the racing yachts. But at 12.15 p.m. on Saturday, 2 September 1989, the starting cannon was fired by the Duke of Edinburgh, Prince Philip, from the Royal Yacht Squadron, an exclusive part of the upper-echelons of English sailing, and the twenty-three yachts began their race.

NCB Ireland, IR 1992 her sail number, crossed the line with Joe English from Cobh in charge. He had taken over as skipper at a late stage due to internal personnel problems. It was a tough and pressurised task to take control so close to the start of a 32,000-mile ocean challenge. His brother, Eddie, another well-known and experienced south coast sailor, was co-commentator with me.

Some yachts were boxed in by the spectator fleet, which broke protocols to keep them away from the start line. Overhead the skies were crowded with helicopters, an airship, and even Aer Lingus's veteran De Havilland biplane *Iolar*, literally flying the flag for *NCB Ireland*.

My over-riding memory of that day is the huge wash kicked up by all the boats moving, the waves powering into the shore where we were in the cabins. At one stage, as we described the start, Eddie closed the window against the spray from the boats, mixed with the wind-driven spray and the rising sea, even though there was a sunny blue sky of a September afternoon.

After the boats left and our commentary finished, a quietness came down, a feeling of being a little deflated after the excitement of the start and the broadcast. I thought of the crew facing into their first night at sea, an experience I had often had on races, wondering what lay ahead. Little did I know that when *NCB Ireland* returned to British waters for the finish, I would be aboard as one of the crew.

As the race progressed, I followed it, reporting regularly into the main television sports programme on RTÉ 1 – Saturday afternoon's *Sports Stadium*. I arranged to get footage from *NCB* through the race organisers and sponsors, plus film by the crew onboard the boat. It was the first race where such video coverage was attempted. There were fixed cameras on the mast and the stern and one mobile camera, linked to a recorder below decks with basic editing facilities. There was a red button in the cockpit on deck which, I learned when aboard, was called the 'panic button' and was pressed whenever there was something worthwhile to film or if the boat was hitting some difficulties.

NCB Ireland did not perform as well as hoped, despite the skill, abilities and hard work of the crew. But they performed some heroics. I remember getting a call at home in Cork one lunchtime when the boom, holding the bottom of the mainsail, had broken, a huge problem. This had happened at 9 p.m. on 9 November when the wind speed was about twenty-five knots and *NCB* was keeping pace with the leaders. The crew turned to and, naming themselves the 'Howling Fifties Spar Team', they made a repair which kept the boat going. It was no easy task repairing a boom the size of *NCB's* on an eighty-one-foot boat.

The boom broke a second time, in the Southern Ocean, the toughest ocean in the world and not a place anyone would want difficulties aboard a yacht and again at a bad time, close to midnight in twenty-five to twenty-eight knots of wind. Again the crew overcame the problem, continuing with a loose-footed mainsail, a development that was ahead of its time in sailing. They also overcame a third break. These were determined sailors, not all of Irish origin, but of international reputation and recruited to the Irish boat for their abilities.

One of the world's top sailors, until his untimely death, was Peter Blake, who skippered *Steinlager*, the New Zealand ketch which won the race. It was the only ketch and flew an extra sail at the stern, and overpowered every other yacht in the race, which then did not demand a single design of racing yacht to enter.

In Fort Lauderdale, where I joined *NCB*, Blake told me:

'Your Irish guys do what others of us would hardly attempt to keep the boat moving. They are a great bunch on *NCB* and I'm proud to be on this race with them. They don't whinge and they don't moan about what has happened to the boat. They get on with the job, even though we all know, everyone on every boat in this race knows, that they have a slow boat.'

The crew themselves were calling *NCB* 'the Lead Sled', though they retained a love and admiration for her, as all mariners do for the vessel on which they live and work. No matter how it might have performed, there was a pride in their boat. Back in Ireland there was no such pride amongst the multitude of critics. There were begrudgers about the money spent and the media generally did not help. There was a press backlash against *NCB Ireland* and the entire project was called into question.

I felt differently. I fought against this attitude and while reporting with the balance which journalism requires, I continually made the point that the crew were out in the toughest of conditions, facing the worst that the oceans could throw at them, and they had overcome it in the best spirit of determination that Ireland could be proud of. These guys were representing Ireland proudly and from every port they went to there were positive reports of the Irish boat and the Tricolour flying from the stern.

As I write these words now, it reminds me that I fought the same battle over the *Jeanie Johnston* many years later. There always seems to be begrudgery and a negative media where maritime matters are concerned. The Irish media were quick to run bad news about *NCB Ireland*, but slow to praise the crew or anything they did or achieved. There were self-serving reporters and columnists who thought up 'smart' things to write, using the initials *NCB* to coin phrases such as 'Never Coming Back' and 'Nice Cruising Boat'.

From September through the autumn, into the winter, and then the approach of spring, the 32,000-mile race with its calls to ports around the world still continued in its nine-month challenge. The race reached Punta del Este in Uruguay and was due to re-start from there in March 1990 for the next leg to Fort Lauderdale in the United States. A few weeks before, I was invited to a lunch at NCB offices in Dublin and there too was another reporter, Gerry Byrne, who covered sailing for the *Sunday Tribune*. We were told that it had been decided to offer two places to sail on the last two legs aboard *NCB*. This was an attempt to reverse the bad publicity and it seemed that we were the only two reporters giving the project balanced coverage.

I agreed to go, as did Gerry, but the choice of legs went to a toss of a coin which Gerry won and he selected the leg to Fort Lauderdale. I was left with the final leg across the Atlantic from Fort Lauderdale to Southampton, which, I was told, would be 'a microcosm' of the entire race, with all the varying conditions encountered. So it proved to be.

It was April 1990 when I arrived in Fort Lauderdale to join the yacht. I had flown out with Maurice Reidy, RTÉ Television Sports Producer for *Sports Stadium*. He had a return airline ticket. Mine was one-way: my passage home was to be on the water. We spent about two weeks filming interviews and recording stories with every one of the yachts still left in the race, while the *NCB* crew rested up and then began preparations for the next leg, on which I would be joining them.

During that period I was concerned about the possibility of sea sickness and seeming a fool in front of the professional crew, so I set out in search of a remedy – an impossible mission as most sailors will testify to. Most people suffer at some stage from *mal de mer*. If you are to get it you will. The only foolproof remedy is to stay ashore. But I got advice that patches could be placed behind the ear, which would help with balance by leaching a chemical into the bloodstream. These were only available on medical prescription, but a visit to a pharmacy, a pleading story about my sailing participation and using the Irish legendary association of the emigrant in the foreign, but favourable, land, worked and I got the patches – and a reputation. When I rang home in the regular contact with my wife Kathleen, who to her credit backed me in sailing with *NCB* and was caring for our four children back at home, she wanted to know what I was doing having 'studs' put in my ears!

I hadn't.

'The *Gay Byrne Hour* said you had.'

The radio programme had sent a reporter to Fort Lauderdale, but somehow the reality and the report were at odds with each other and my story about the ear patches had become ear studs to avoid sea sickness!

There was another misunderstanding – between myself and the skipper under whom I would be crewing across the Atlantic. Amid the opulence of Fort Lauderdale and the brash 'if you have it, flaunt it' attitudes of the Americans, many parties were held and the sailors were the centre of a lot of social attention. At one Irish-American supporters' club party for the *NCB* crew, I strolled into the Club 66 reception, in a room which was adjacent to the media centre, in which I had been doing work on my report back to RTÉ about the *NCB*. I was in my 'working attire' of trousers, shirt, even a tie, as I talked to some *NCB* crew members in the sunshine of a Florida evening. There was a bit of distance with them, which I needed to overcome, because they had a pretty strong disaffection towards journalists. Joe English came over to me and, in front of the crew members, said:

'What do you think you're doing?'

My answer, that I was having a drink with some of the crew, was answered with:

'You're not wearing a crew shirt. You signed onto the crew, didn't you? [I had at the race office in accordance with race regulations]. Are you a crew member now or a journalist? You agreed to crew the boat and I expect you to show that.'

English was showing his authority. It was a clash immediately between me and him, which the crew were watching. Time for me to choose. I was either with them as part of the crew or staying on the sidelines.

'Sorry, nothing meant.'

I hurried back into the media centre, to find my bag where I had the gear needed and quickly slipped into the shirt and returned to the reception. Joe English was across the room, but glanced my way and saw the change of attire, so did the crew. The skipper's authority had been accepted. Anyway, I'd have to sail with these guys to get home safely!

Maurice Reidy had set off back to Ireland with all his programme tapes and I was on familiarisation sailing with the crew in the days before the race re-start. My future lay in the sea route, so I had better get used to it. Joe English made his authority known with sharpness, crankiness. I saw it all and began to wonder at times if I was going to sail under some sort of tyranny. Joining the crew's rented accommodation in the few days leading up to the re-start it was clear that I was the lowest of the rankings, bunking in a sleeping bag on a sofa or the floor of an apartment. During practice sailing before the restart I was put on the grinder, probably keeping me as much out of the way as possible. It is an instrument of torture if you are not fully up-to-scratch, as you wind first one way and then the other with a companion at the other side of the 'infernal equipment' as it seemed to be.

The morning of the race was an early start – 5 a.m. I wasn't feeling so good, a mixture of fear and apprehension gnawing at my stomach. Joe English led the crew to a restaurant for breakfast by 7 a.m. and they all ate heartily. Not me! Facing the Atlantic was something I was not very happy about at this stage, added to which I was suffering from a few severely bruised ribs, sustained while sailing round the Fastnet Rock in West Cork in late March in rough weather to prepare for the Atlantic, not to mention the after effects of the 'grinder'.

What the hell was I doing? I was forty-four. I would be the oldest crewman and had the least experience of deep-ocean racing.

By 9 a.m. Joe had taken *NCB Ireland* off its berth at Pier 66 and we were standing out into the river, waiting for the road bridge to rise to allow us access to open water. I must have looked the most anguished and concerned member of the crew! I had been told to expect thirty-, forty- and fifty-knot headwinds in what would be arduous, even 'appalling' seas, depending upon who was speaking to me at the time.

I couldn't turn back now.

On the start line I was again put on the grinder, at least I knew what that did. The excitement was tremendous all round, with huge numbers of boats on the water and spectators everywhere. The American Coast Guard, not a group of seafarers renowned for courtesy and understanding, decided to bring a vessel right across the start line. It didn't matter to them if this was the start of a round-the-world race: this was what they did and they would bludgeon their way through where they wanted to go.

With the usual roaring and shouting, the race started and after a while we threw overboard in a watertight, floating bag my first television report off the yacht, to be picked up by a following boat and forwarded to RTÉ. A few hours later came a headsail change and I was sent up the bow with other crew members to change sail. I learned the power of the Atlantic as compared to Cork harbour and the south coast as I turned my back to the breakers coming over the bow. I was swept back half the length of the eighty-one-foot boat, picking myself up bruised and a bit battered.

I shared a 'hot bunk' with Watch Leader Terry Gould. It meant that we shared the same bunk when off-watch. I rolled out of it when he called me on deck: he did the same when it was my turn to rest. There was a 'watch' system which kept us on duty for at least fourteen hours out of every twenty-four and more if the need arose. It took a fair deal of time to get in and out of the layers of clothing required when it was cold. At times, up near the Labrador Banks, as we watched for icebergs, when you took your socks off they would go hard from the damp and sweat.

I learned to live on freeze-dried food that tasted like elastic bands at times – the wondrous delight of a bar of chocolate. I queued for my food in front of the galley that was barely the size of a telephone box, presenting my plastic bowl into which every kind of food went when it was cooked. The bowl was wiped clean as fast as possible for what came next. I made coffee and tea, washed utensils, did everything I was asked, and tried to fit in as a member of the crew.

I watched for icebergs. I twice tore the skipper's coffee cup from its pride of place in a container at the side of the navigation station as I fell out of my bunk, trying to get to the floor to go on duty, when the yacht was heeled well over.

I was asked 'what kind of an idiot' I was, but I kept my opinions to myself. I showered in cold buckets of water on the stern, was glad when a chance came to get to the 'heads' – the toilet without a door up in the bow – shaved if I had the chance to keep myself clear, every few days.

I lost over half a stone in weight and fell through the galley hatch on the roof, which formed part of the floor of the deck, but about which I had not been told and which had been left open in the dark. It was very painful when one leg went through the opening, right up to my personal vital organs. I managed to drag myself back up, while hauling the long, heavy sails and zipping them into bags to be put away below decks. My leg, thigh and part of my backside sported a huge, multi-coloured bruise that added to my already sore ribs. I could barely climb into my bunk, two-up, a piece of canvas spread between to poles, but it was a place to rest when I got there.

I didn't tell anyone, but naval Lieutenant Bob McCarthy, the medic aboard, spotted the injury when I was changing and gave me pain-killers. We sailed on, varying between good and bad weather, a huge thunderstorm lighting up the sky at one stage, absolute flat water with no wind at others so we floated in the middle of the Atlantic Ocean, barely moving. We heard on the yacht's daily radio schedule as it reported progress that we were near the front, then had slipped back.

At three o'clock on a dark Atlantic morning, with the wind blowing strongly, Bowman Guy Barron heard a different noise from the boat, above all the other regular noises, and shouted a warning – the portside runner, taking the strain of the elements, was about to give and that would threaten the mast and could bring the rig down. There was a sudden, quick gybe to take the pressure off and put it on the starboard runner supporting the mast. We were not going the right way any longer, but the rig had been saved.

In heavy-weather gear I was leaning out over the stern a short time later, holding onto the rail with one hand and using a torch to help with the repair with the other. I felt that if I went over the side that would be the end of me. Even with lifesaving gear you would be swept away in no time, into the darkness, the only illumination being from the 'white horses' on the Atlantic rollers. Another repair was made in a makeshift workshop below decks which, as well as eating and sleeping accommodation, held a sewing machine for sail repairs and all our weather gear. There wasn't much space, but in it the crew used chain to fashion a repair, which was then rigged to the mast, and a repair down to a spreader, which was also looking dodgy under the pressure stress of racing. I admired these guys for their determination. They did not know, nor did they recognise, the thought of giving up. The phrase didn't have a place in their minds.

Along the way I had to give reports, when contact was possible and facilities allowed, to RTÉ and for *Seascapes* – then being presented by one of my colleagues, Antoin O'Callaghan, while I was on the high seas.

Lying in my bunk near the stern of *NCB Ireland*, with air coming through the open stern area and down from the deck, where there was no closed area between the cockpit and the below-decks crew accommodation, it could be cold at times, warm at others, depending upon the climate in which we were sailing at the time. With my feet always forward to take the shock as the boat ploughed into waves or hit what the crew jocosely called 'pot holes', when she might fall off a wave into a trough, I thought of the critics and begrudgers back in Ireland who had done a hatchet job on *NCB*, probably snug in warm beds that were not being thrown around by high seas, and said to myself – *to blazes with them!*

As I shivered in the cold of the Atlantic at two in the morning and then heard the bang of a spinnaker blowing out, the call came from the Watch Leader:

'Come on you guys, get that kite down and changed, we're still racing.'

With the others on watch duty, it was time to go forward out of the comparative safety of the cockpit onto the heaving, bouncing deck, dragging a heavy sail bag forward, helping winch the bowman up the 118-foot mast to get the torn part of the kite down and re-rig for the new one. The new one was set flying quickly and trimmed, while the damaged parts were brought below decks where sailmaker Robbie Naismith was standing by to begin repair work and get it ready for use again.

We kept pace with the remaining boats, then fell back to tenth or eleventh place, fighting a fierce battle with *Gatorade* from Italy, but so close that the crew of *NCB* would not give up in their fight for even one place down the fleet.

The night before the finish was magical, as we sailed south of Ireland towards Southampton. As we reported our position to Race Control, the transmissions were picked up by Irish fishing boats, by cargo ships, by ferries, by the navy and wherever there was an Irish seafarer: good wishes were sent and we were congratulated for getting back. These were men who understood what being at sea meant, who did not share the begrudgery of the national media or the critics of the project. I felt proud to be a part of this crew. There were tears of emotion in my eyes as I heard a fisherman out of Union Hall, a good West Cork port, call: 'Good on you lads. Up the Irish! Never say die …Welcome back to Irish waters …' Others radioed: 'Go for it you guys' and 'Great stuff … Well done *NCB Ireland*.'

It raised the spirits, the morale of the crew, and *NCB* seemed to me to lift herself clearer of the water, to raise her bow to speed herself towards the finish at Southampton. As we made towards there in the early hours of the morning, Joe English had all the crew up on deck with orders to make sure our tacks (changes of direction of the yacht when the sails are set in a new direction) were top-class, that there were no mistakes made as we came within reach of the media out of Southampton, who would be recording our finish. He told his crew that they had done a good, professional job, that they had come through a long voyage together, and said to me: 'You've done OK. You're one of us.'

The arrival in Southampton was magical. Irish team support boats came down the Solent flying Tricolours. The British army fired the finishing-line cannon, and the Irish national anthem was played as we came into the finishing berth and lines were thrown ashore. *NCB* was home and so was I, but only partially so.

It was a Friday: next day was a *Sports Stadium* transmission. It was also early – around 6.30 a.m. I had radio broadcasts to do for RTÉ News; then off with the crew for a long, leisurely breakfast in the race village; then to a hotel and a resting sleep. I had to bid them farewell. I have always regretted missing that very special time when, as a crew which has bonded together during a voyage, you relax and celebrate. For me, the journalistic role now resumed.

I bade farewell to Joe English. 'My job takes over and it's the only way you guys will be recognised for what you have done,' I told him as I left hurriedly, bound for a taxi to the Southampton coach station and a direct bus straight into Heathrow for a flight to Dublin. There were a few rows with security over the video tapes as the X-ray machines at airports were not totally safe where these tapes were concerned. At one stage I was told I would not be allowed fly, at another that I would be arrested and removed from the airport. But, thankfully, arrangements were made and I got back to Dublin and into TV editing in time to put a package together overnight and into the following morning for the last part of the *NCB Ireland* story.

Ireland's first entry in the round-the-world yacht race had faced dangers, hardship and mishap, which had been faced with courage, tenacity and skill.

This is what seafarers do, often out of sight, out of mind of those ashore.

36

FROM STEAMSHIPS AND CABLES
TO THE ROUND IRELAND

There is a nice walk along Wicklow Harbour's southern quayside, past the sailing club and the lifeboat station, where you can look back at the town and the commercial berthage for the harbour. On the walls are paintings of many boats which have called to Wicklow, an unusual pictorial record that makes it attractive and where the yachts berth for the Round Ireland Race. It is the biggest race in Ireland, providing a unique opportunity to sail non-stop around a nation, and it is considered a jewel in the international racing crown. That a small club from a small port should run it is a tribute to those who first devised the idea, though Wicklow has had to fight off the clutches of other clubs in larger locations who would love to have it in their sailing schedule. This gives Wicklow a particular place in Irish sailing.

The club was founded in 1950 at a meeting held in the town's Bridge Hotel, which was the birthplace of the famous Captain Robert Halpin, Master of the *Great Eastern* steamship that laid the first transatlantic cable in the late 1860s . The late Joseph T. O'Byrne (fondly remembered by all as J. T.) is credited in the town as 'the guiding arm of the club's formation.'

The club's first boats had an interesting history. The members decided on the Cadet, a twelve-foot wooden dinghy, and the first five of these came from an unlikely source. A former army captain, who had killed his wife's lover in a fit of jealous rage, was detained in what was then known as the Dundrum Lunatic Asylum for the Criminally Insane and was contracted by the founding members to build a number of these boats. Along with the unfortunate captain's consignment, collected from Dundrum by Harry Jordan (a founding member, former commodore and WSC's only continuous member for over fifty years), other members acquired or built boats and created a racing fleet of dinghies. But Wicklow had more to give.

Wicklow had a long history of Cruiser racing going back to the previous century, when the British custodians of the day would run regattas in conjunction with the Town Regatta Festival, which is Ireland's oldest continuously-run festival, for their military and 'noble folk'. Some of their 'grand trophies' have survived to the present day. In more modern times, several regattas and rallies, using Wicklow as their hub, attracted sailors from up and down the coast, as well as from Wales and England. This gave club members the idea of creating something new and unique in national and international racing.

The late Michael Jones suggested that WSC should organise a race, starting from and finishing in Wicklow, leaving Ireland and all its islands to starboard, so the Round Ireland was born in 1980 and Michael was the organiser for many years. I have sat in his race office which is perched above the harbour wall at Wicklow, with his successor, the Co-ordinator Denis Noonan and club members who provide a twenty-four-hour watch during the race. Boats may finish at any time. For the 2008 race they introduced a new development, a website tracking facility so that the position of boats could be seen by the public around the coast at any time. It was innovative, helpful for both safety and for the families of those crewing on boats to know where they were positioned.

'We intend to continue to run the Round Ireland for the foreseeable future,' the members told me when we broadcast *Seascapes* live from their clubhouse during the 2008 Race. They are looking to expand sailing and boating on the coast, but like many clubs are finding space to moor boats limited, as more people buy vessels and seek places to keep them. 'Unfortunately, space is now at a serious premium and we are unable to provide space for new boatowners.'

The club's newsletter said:

> *Perhaps the initiatives of bodies like the Irish Marine Federation, who represent leisure boating interests against a Government that continues to ignore Ireland's potential maritime goldmine, will bear fruit as there seems to be a severe lack of will in the Public Service sector to improve Wicklow's long overdue upgrade to a promised marina location.*

37

FOUR DAYS OR THE IRON RATIONS

The Royal Cork Yacht Club is the oldest in the world, tracing its history back to 1720, the earliest days of sail boat racing. There are those who have, over the years, disputed the club's claim, but it remains undiminished and, over its many years, it has contributed great sailors to Ireland's maritime history.

When I joined the club at Crosshaven I was in awe of legendary names like Denis Doyle, who owned and sailed the Frers 51 wooden *Moonduster*, another legend in sailing.

Denis Doyle ran one of the biggest companies involved in the shipping industry in Cork. He was involved in the stevedoring business, companies which have dock labour forces, unloading ships. It can be a tough business; dockers were known as hard men, working in what could be harsh conditions even for their day, unloading ships, though containerisation and modern dockside equipment has changed much of that and the days of traditional dock labour seem to be numbered.

But, amongst Cork dockers, there was an interest in sailing and particularly in Denis's legendary *Moonduster* and how it performed. Denis Doyle was clearly the man in charge, who sailed in all weathers, all conditions and *Moonduster* made her mark throughout Europe even, it was reported, on a legendary occasion when the King of Spain asked to meet Denis and see his boat.

'Legendary' is a word easily attached to Denis Doyle, who, when I first went sailing, was helpful to me as a newcomer, willing to give advice, to talk, to encourage. I admired and like him, but he was not an easy many to get to do an interview, being of few words when a microphone was produced. He set records, including the speed record for the Round Ireland Yacht Race, the non-stop 704-nautical mile race that is one of the world's classics. It stood for many years and it took modern yachts, stripped-out, specially-built racing boats with as little weight and as much sails as possible – far from the solid, heavy build of *Moonduster* – to beat the Doyle record.

Every two years I would try for an interview as *Moonduster* was prepared in Wicklow harbour for the start of the race run by Wicklow Harbour Sailing Club. Denis would be courteous, but not always available when I returned to the boat with my camera crew and radio recorder, having established earlier that he was around.

I did get him on a few occasions, but he never spoke much about himself, or wanted to highlight his sailing achievements. Denis enjoyed his sport and what the boat won, and being a member of his crew was a privileged position. Many members of the Naval Service crewed with Denis.

He introduced hundreds of youngsters to sailing on his various craft down through the years and, competitive and successful to the day he died, he took part in the Winter League series in the RCYC until his death.

Moonduster was big and needed space and depth and, at times in close quarters in Cork, dinghies could get in the way! But he didn't lose his composure even then. I saw *Moonduster* in the narrow confines of the upper reaches of the River Lee off Passage during the annual Cobh to Blackrock Race when a twelve-foot Mirror dinghy with two young sailors out of the Royal Cork called starboard on the towering and powering *Moonduster* as it came upriver at them. Being on starboard gives you rights of way, but the dinghy and its two young sailors were up against a fifty-one-footer and a crew of more than twelve. The call was made in a voice that seemed to pipe up from below *Moonduster*; a little tremulously it called "Starboard ... starboard ..." Then, more urgently: "ah ... starboard Mr Doyle ..."

Moonduster came around in a racing turn executed by the crew, the little dinghy passed in front, *Moonduster* swiftly came back in course and powered on, leaving the little dinghy in its wake and two youngsters talking to each other:

'Did you see that, *Moonduster* turned for us?'

'I didn't think he would."

'Mr Doyle would, he knows the rules.'

The rules of interviewing might be a little different, if there are any, but there was no calling 'starboard' on Denis to get him to face the camera. But there was Mary, his redoubtable wife, who was looking after the provisioning of her husband's steed when I came upon her during preparations for one of the Round Ireland races.

She was ticking off a list of what had gone aboard for the crew's food requirements; still not loaded was a collection of tins of steak and kidney pie.

Mary was checking the fresh food that had gone on, everything was being ticked off. I asked her how long she thought the race would take, how many days the boat was being provisioned for. I wanted to include her and this scene in the sports programme we were making for the race. She estimated that the *Duster*, as it was popularly known, should be back in about three days, four at the most. She would expect that of her husband.

'If it isn't,' she said, as Denis emerged from the boat to do his promised interview and waving at the tins of steak and kidney – 'it's the iron rations.'

That year, we called the programme about the race – 'Four Days or the Iron Rations'.

I remember the day during winter league racing in Cork when *Moonduster* lost her mast. I was crewing on a boat just rounding Ringabella course mark outside Cork Harbour, and we were going onto a 'run' – the point of sailing where spinnakers are hauled up at the bow of the yacht. For the spectator these can be described as those lovely, coloured sails, but in difficult conditions they can be difficult to handle and, on occasion, sailors describe a boat in rolling conditions with a spinnaker or 'kite' up as it is called, as 'yellow pants time'.

As boats rounded the mark, often close together, side-by-side, skippers roared for the spinnakers to be hauled, then some saw the mast of *Moonduster* up ahead, as she regularly was, crumple and fall.

Never did I hear more skippers shouting: 'don't haul, don't haul, don't haul …' and crews flinging themselves across spinnakers to stop them going up.

Moonduster could set the pattern in many ways!

One of my friends in sailing is W. M. Nixon, known to sailing enthusiasts as 'Winkie Nixon', himself a renowned sailor, wrote a tribute to Denis in his sailing column in the *Irish Independent*:

It is as though the Fastnet Rock has suddenly, inexplicably and totally disappeared from its unique position off the coast of West Cork. The unexpected death of the great Denis Doyle on Sunday is an event of incomprehensible magnitude. Just as the Fastnet Rock is the symbol of the Irish coast at its most inspiring, so Denis Doyle was the very personification of Irish deep sea racing at its best for the global sailing community. You might well think that when a man has led a long and fruitful life and was still sailing in his 81st year within days of his death, that the predominant reaction would be one of wonder and celebration that he had achieved so much and been so active to the very end. But this week, the sombre reality of Denis Doyle's funeral has left the Irish and world sailing community with a feeling of numbness. He was a man with no airs or graces, almost a shy man, yet he touched so many lives by his inspiration and example and help and simple friendliness he is very genuinely mourned and missed. His sailing career was extraordinary. It went on for decades, and it was a measure of the man that he never stopped learning, never lost his zest and enthusiasm.

Denis Doyle was of the generation which expected owners to helm their own racing boats, but he was prepared to use specialist helmsmen, if he felt they could get the best out of his boats during a particular campaign. But even as he reached his eighties, Denis would take the helm for hours himself, in the particular position he liked at the stern. In tough, survival conditions, he would be there when the weather was not for yachting, but a place for special sailors – of which Denis Doyle was undoubtedly one.

38

LOVE AT SEA – THE *MAB*

'You've been round here twice already … If you come around again, I'll send for the Guards …'

It was the only time in my life that I have been threatened with possible arrest at sea. Though I wasn't sure that the Gardaí would have any transport immediately available to them in Glandore Harbour.

My skipper urged caution:

'Shssh … No names now in case she hear us, row on … Tom.'

The Skipper had no problem in disclosing my name in that early morning hour across Glandore Harbour as the somewhat irate woman withdrew her head from the opening between the cockpit and the boat's cabin. But skippers are superior people to crew. They give orders, they have an authority on their boats, so I didn't reply, just rowed away in the inflatable with my skipper happily clutching his prizes to his chest. I knew that he needed me to get him back to his floating home, the nautical joy of his life. Crews *really* know whether things are at – or in my case on this occasion, wished they did! We were being as quiet as possible while trying, with increasing desperation, to find the *Mab* in the semi-darkness of the hour just after midnight.

This 1913 sloop was the focus of our lives that weekend. But she had a rather low freeboard, so was not easy to see amongst the many yachts in the harbour. Thoughts about liberal celebrations of victory at the Glandore Classic Boats Gathering having an inhibiting effect are not to be entertained.

We were both clad in protective gear and lifejackets as I rowed the inflatable – known as *The Blob* because it had originally served as tender to one of my former boats, called *Scribbler*. Passing the end of the pier at the inner part of Glandore Harbour, we headed for the *Mab*, but she proved elusive. There were so many yachts in the anchorage area that summer evening that we could not easily locate her. As the occasional, gentle wave rippled underneath the inflatable and carried us onward, boat after boat was passed, without success, until the angry lady decided we had been round hers a few times – unbeknownst to us it might be added. Maybe she suspected thieves! A few minutes later we saw our target – there was the *Mab*, exactly where we had left her and onto which I pushed skipper and his trophies, without the Gardaí in hot pursuit.

Crewing for the same skipper regularly either leads to disagreement and separation or a long-lasting bond of friendship. In my case, it was making a great friend.

Guy Perrem owned the classic yacht, *Mab*, which he had come across when she was in a pretty bad condition, as he described her. He spent time, effort and money, lavishing care on a boat in which he had great pride. She dated from 1913, had survived being blown ashore in a gale in Courtmacsherry Bay, but appeared to have lost love and support until Guy happened across her. From that day, she survived and Guy loved his wooden boat.

Every two years there would be an 'overseas' voyage, as it was jokingly called, to get her from Monkstown Bay to Glandore

Harbour for the Traditional Boats Gathering, where Guy would announce his arrival in a spectacular way. A modern power boat would cover that distance in a few hours. For the *Mab*, it could take a day or two – or more – including a stop-over in Kinsale along the way!

More often than not, I was Guy's crew and the two of us would set about the task, accompanied on some occasions by Guy's wife, Breda, and other members of our local Monkstown Bay Sailing Club, the village where we lived. All of the villagers, like the rest of Guy's family, accorded the *Mab* and its needs a special place in life.

On one windy night, with a lively sea, a few miles past Cork Harbour's impressive entrance of Roche's Point and the forts of Carlisle and Camden, Guy and myself sat in the small cockpit of the *Mab*. She was about twenty-eight feet long, with her bowsprit adding to the overall length and, as the waves advanced towards her, the *Mab* would from time-to-time not lift herself over them. The bowsprit would poke straight into the wave, reminding me of an old lady with threatening knitting needles, ready to puncture the bulk of an aggressor. So the waves would slap over the hull and run down the sides of the narrow cockpit, sitting inside which we were fortunately protected from the water by the high coaming sides.

'She has seen all of this before Tom,' Guy would cheerfully say. 'You can't expect an old lady of the sea to lift her skirts to every little upstart of a wave that challenges her … Straight through she'll go – that's experience.'

And so she would, as we ploughed into another wave.

Occasionally, with her big headsail and a tall mast – which I once had to climb when I mistakenly pulled a halyard to the top, as a result realising just how tall it was – we would have to turn on the engine to bring her bow around in a tack. And, regularly, bailing would be needed as she took some water between the planks below decks.

'Wooden boats are like that, they need to seal up, she'll be fine, is it your turn to bail for a while, the pump will do it,' skipper Guy would intone as he puffed on a cigarette or checked the GPS, one of the modern pieces of navigational equipment which he enjoyed using.

The *Mab* had unusual markings, which distinguished her from any other boat I have ever been on. She had two 'coffin pieces' cut into the mast, which recalled two of her former owners who had drowned. Guy's legendary stories about the *Mab* also held that she had been on her way out of Irish waters in 1939, carrying her then owners on an intended holiday, when she was stopped by a British naval vessel and advised to return home, because the Second World War had started and a small vessel like her would not be safe in waters which were about to become very hostile.

She did not have a shot fired *at* her, but she had several fired *from* her!

Guy had his own ideas about the 'honour signal' to Glandore, which became part of the tradition of the boat, as the *Mab* arrived for the Traditional Boats Gathering held every two years in the West Cork port. Just off the small, rocky islands of Adam and Eve near the harbour entrance – boats are warned to 'avoid Adam and hug Eve', no doubt from sad experience – the honour ceremony of arrival would begin.

Guy would go below deck and emerge back in the cockpit with his shotgun. All perfectly legally held it should be stated, lest anyone consider the Gardaí should once again be needed to call to us. Two shots would be discharged into the air. The sound would be heard in the Glandore Inn, centre of sailing in the village, and the word would go out 'the *Mab* is coming'.

We had great sailing times in Glandore and, to Guy's great delight, the *Mab* would be in the prizes at every event.

There was the year when, approaching a starboard mark on the racing course, we were getting quite close to it. The rules prevent boats from touching marks of the course. To do so incurs a penalty. Ron Holland from Kinsale, another friend of Guy's, was on the helm and called for a tack. This would be a turn to get the boat onto a new course – because we were too close to the mark. But it could mean losing time to the boats behind, which might catch up and pass us. Guy, who always knew just what the *Mab* was capable of, called those of us crewing for him to get ready. We were all from Monkstown Bay Sailing Club and had the club burgee flying from the stern to denote our birthright – Chris Granby, Don Teegan, myself. As we closed the mark, on Guy's instruction we grabbed and lifted the long, heavy boom which ran out to the stern of the boat. Guy shouted at Ron to make the turn, the *Mab* pivoted, the boom went over the top of the mark and Guy shouted to drop it again. It cleared over the mark perfectly!

'There you are,' said Guy. 'The rules say a boat mustn't touch the mark, we never did.' Clearly Guy knew the rules better than anyone else!

It is said that around the entrance to Glandore, waves occasionally produce a keening sound, which you might be told locally is the 'Tonn Chliodhna' or 'Cliona's Wave'. Legend has it that in the distant past a love-sick young girl drowned in this area and the keening is her ghostly lament. A more realistic explanation is that, in certain conditions of wind and tide, the keening sound is produced by the wind echoing in the crevices and caves in the cliffs.

We were in those waves during one of the Classic events. It was heavy weather for the *Mab*, with rough waves accompanied by a pretty high wind. These were tough conditions for older boats a mile south of Glandore, but then the *Mab* lifted those skirts of hers to which Guy referred and began to outpace boats of a younger vintage. With her big mainsail and the wind abeam – coming over the centre/side of the boat, which is the fastest point of sailing known as 'reaching' – she was making seven to eight knots. Her average was around three to four knots.

'She's above her hull speed, she is really travelling,' Guy whooped in delight as we surged down the waves. But the rest of us were concerned because we could see that a mile or so ahead we would have to tack again and go onto a beat, the boat heading directly into the wind and, with the big sail, we would be over-canvassed and need to reef down, reduce the sail size.

We wanted to reef down the mainsail, but the skipper calls the shots and Guy was in seven-knot heaven.

'Keep her going, look at that,' Guy would shout, as his GPS showed a speed the *Mab* had never reached before and she passed out another of the modern 'plastic' boats as Guy called them, those made of GRP – glassfibre reinforced polyester.

He was in his element, but the inevitable came as we tacked to beat into the wind. It was not the point of sailing in which the *Mab* revelled. She began to pound up and down, there was a tearing sound and the headsail was damaged. Undaunted, Guy sent Rowan, my son, also crewing, forward with a replacement that was attached and the *Mab* continued her slog to the finish. But we heard another bang as she rose on a wave and slapped down. She was damaged underneath, something had given and she began to take water, so there was more bailing and she had to be grounded at the pier inside Glandore Harbour. This meant drying her out as the tide fell. Liam Hegarty came out from Oldcourt in Skibbereen, where he runs a yard that has a particular specialty in dealing with old boats. The *Mab* was patched underneath for her return home, accompanied by even more bailing.

She continued to make her presence known back in Cork and, nothing daunted, showing great commitment to his wooden boat, Guy decided on an extensive refurbishment at Liam Hegarty's yard. She repaid this at the next Glandore Traditional Classics. Before the event I joined Guy at the yard, from where we took her down the lovely River Ilen, with the kind guidance of the Baltimore-Sherkin Island ferry, which was also returning from a visit there. After a stay at Baltimore, the next stop was Glandore, with Guy's brother, Tom, and other crew joining and where, again, the *Mab* resumed her triumphal presence.

It was not long after lavishing such care and attention on the *Mab* that Guy died suddenly. He left my house one evening after sailing, heading home. The next morning I was driving to an assignment in Dublin when a phone call told me that Guy had died suddenly during the night.

So, I stood with fellow club members at the flagstaff at Monkstown Bay Sailing Club at the edge of Cork Harbour as we dipped the club's ensign and fired the race starting cannons in honour and tribute to Guy as his cortège passed by.

My friend, my wooden boat skipper, had sailed for the last time.

39

GHOSTLY DUNMORE EAST

On Thursday night, 11 January 2007, I fought tears of emotion from my eyes as I stood on the steps of the Fishermen's Co-op in Dunmore East in County Waterford, looking out across the cold night, seeing people on the harbour wall looking hopelessly out to sea. All that was to be seen on the dark, cold, rolling waters, with a heavy swell pounding towards the harbour walls, were the navigation lights of vessels still out on the sea, lifted occasionally on the white wave tops. They were looking for missing fishermen, whose bodies had not been found after the sinking of two trawlers, the *Pere Charles* from Dunmore itself and the *Honey Dew II* from Kinsale in County Cork.

There were seven fishermen dead out there and it was the only night when I introduced *Seascapes* without the theme music 'Sailing By', by which the programme is widely known. There was an unusual atmosphere hanging over the port it seemed to me. There was a sense of eeriness – it seemed at times to have a ghostly, quiet atmosphere as people waited for something to happen, yet this quiet mixed peculiarly with the hum of generators aboard fishing boats. Families waited in hope that was never realised, that the men might be found. Tears welled up in my eyes. This was not, I told myself, how an experienced broadcaster should feel, but I could not help myself and, inside the Co-op as the broadcast continued and I looked around the table where we were sitting, at the faces of other fishermen, lifeboatmen and the broadcast engineers, I knew that everyone felt the same.

This was a hard night, but much tougher on the families who had lost fathers, brothers and sons. There were fishermen who had come from abroad in search of work and found jobs on the local boats. As crew, they and their families had become part of the fishing communities. Dunmore East and Kinsale, two fishing ports, maritime communities, separated by many miles of coastline, were united in grief. People from Kinsale had come to Waterford to search the coastline with the local people.

Earlier that evening on RTÉ 6/1 TV News I had spoken about how I felt. I had been pretty blunt; I had said the fishermen lost their lives because they were doing what they had to – catching fish to earn a living. There was no doubt in my mind that fishermen were being forced out to sea in bad weather conditions to catch fish because they had to do so to comply with legislation. That had brought strong reaction from right around the country from fishing communities, shocked and deeply concerned by what had happened.

I had met one of the fishermen, Ger Bohan from Kinsale, only a few weeks before, when we had been planning a television report on the problems of the fishing industry, but I had not met him since. I told the public how I felt about fishermen being forced out in the bad weather conditions in which both boats had sunk, by regulations drawn up by bureaucrats who had little or no experience of what life was like at sea fishing; and I raised the question of why the fishermen had died. They died, I said, trying to make a living in the midst of mountains of regulation and bureaucracy.

The men who died in those two tragedies night were:

Aboard the *Pere Charles* –
Pat Hennessy, Tom Hennessy, Billy O'Connor, Andrey Dyrin, Pat Coady

Aboard the *Honey Dew II* –
Ger Bohan, Tomasz Jagly

Any time I go to Dunmore East I stand for a few minutes at the memorial near the waterfront to those who have died at sea. It lists the names of fishermen and seafarers, of an Air Corps crew and of those engaged in leisure activities – all who have shared death on or close to the sea.

John O'Connor wrote a poem which opens:

On misty nights off Dunmore East so the story goes,
Twinkling lights far out at sea shine out in sad repose.
No one knows who they are but the talk is on the quays,
They're the ghosts of long lost ships and men who sailed the seas.

It is an impressive and evocative memorial, alongside which it would take the hardest heart to stand without shedding a tear when reading the list of those who died in marine tragedies.

One of the men who led the establishing of that memorial comes from a family which has been serving Waterford Port for over a hundred years. John Walsh is a former coxswain of the Dunmore East Lifeboat. He became a pilot because of a 'flu epidemic. It was from the port of Rosslare that he first went to sea and on *Seascapes*, he told me about his life, how he became a pilot, of his experiences as a lifeboat coxswain and how he feels deeply for those who have lost their lives in sea tragedies.

John's cousin, Willie, followed him into a seafaring life. Both served first with Irish Shipping, the former state shipping company.

I met John and Willie in Dunmore East Lifeboat Station. They were two men with a deep love of the sea and a proud family tradition, which makes coastal people what they are – the foundation of this island nation. Willie followed John to sea, even though he only washed dishes to start with! Both eventually became Waterford Port Pilots, before they retired.

There are other lines from John O'Connor's poem on the memorial at Dunmore East which resound in my mind:

They'll haul their nets, hoist their sails, set their course no more,
Say a prayer for the souls of the sea who rest just off Dunmore.

There other memorials in other coastal villages and towns which recall occasions of tragedy, with which these areas are only too familiar. I think of Greencastle and Kilmore Quay amongst them as I write these words and there are many others.

Carmel Currid is a great lady, whose husband, Timmy, died in a fishing tragedy. She set up the organisation called LOST (Loved Ones of Sea Tragedies) to help give mutual support to those who have lost relatives at sea. She told me in an interview which I have never forgotten:

'You can never forget that someone went out the door whom you loved and never came back from the sea. That marks you apart. You always remember, you always think of the sea, but you cannot forever blame the sea, you must continue to live, to work on. But you will always think, always remember.'

Her husband, Timmy, died when his fishing boat, the *Scarlet Buccaneer*, was smashed by gales on the outside of the harbour walls at Howth in County Dublin in November 1995, as it tried to get to safety. His heroic radio transmissions as the vessel was in its final moments, alerted the rescue authorities. Howth Lifeboat battled the surging seas to try to get close enough to help in appalling conditions. Efforts were made from the harbour wall to rescue the crew. Two got ashore. A helicopter had to come from the RAF in Wales – it was a time when Ireland could not provide its own cover in such conditions. The RAF rescued another crew member, but Timmy Currid died in hospital after being washed ashore.

It was, regrettably, an example of lack of commitment to the marine sphere that it took disasters to force the provision of adequate rescue requirements. Ireland is now well covered, with rescue helicopters and coastal rescue units, and is even able to provide assistance to UK rescue services.

40

AND SO TO THE FUTURE

Official Ireland has not been good to maritime Ireland, that is unquestionably so. There is a big public interest in the maritime sphere, but its economic possibilities have not been realised as successive Government administrations have reduced its importance within Cabinet. We are an island nation, but Government Departmental structures do not acknowledge the importance of the sea. Ireland has lost economically as a result.

Necessarily this book is a selection taken from hundreds of interviews and stories on *Seascapes*. There are many more, including the boatmen and women of Robertstown with whom I spent a great afternoon as we discussed the Grand Canal and the many boating stories from the years when it was a primary transport route; Clarinbridge and the battle of the oyster fishermen as they struggled to maintain their proud tradition against the onslaught of urban housing and the pollution this threatened to bring to waters which need cleanliness to produce the best oysters which carry Ireland's reputation abroad; the Avoca River, the most polluted in Ireland and how fishery scientists and the local community have been turning that reputation around as the river, passing 'The Meeting of the Waters' made famous by Tom Moore, is cleaned and fish return to it; the building of the tall ship *Dunbrody* in New Ross, County Wexford; the revival and spreading of interest in coastal rowing; the 'sea swimmers' and what they have achieved in making sporting history for Ireland; the traditional boats in the Claddagh and Kinvara; the many fishing companies who keep jobs in coastal areas; those who have developed interest in and protection of whales and dolphins around the Irish coast; the light ships; the ships' radio officers with whom I spent a great night of memories, hilarity and enjoyment as we recorded an hour-long special programme with them; the Guinness barges; the sailing, yacht and boating clubs where I have spent many happy hours with marvellous people; the many islanders I have met and so many, many more people.

There is, as I have said on *Seascapes*, a 'family of the sea', of which as islanders, we are all members.

I hope that those called 'our political masters', though perhaps they should really be regarded as 'our political servants', will put the maritime sphere where it should be – at the top of Irish national affairs.

No man is an island and even though I speak of 'this island nation' every week, neither can I be an island, for the work I do would not have been possible without the many people I have met over my years as a journalist and, for this book and my radio programme on which it is based, without the maritime people who have helped generously with their time and experience and who have come to regard *Seascapes* as a 'voice' for the sea and for marine affairs. To all of them, my deepest thanks, as to my journalistic colleagues over the years and the cameramen, producers, radio technicians, news editors, newsroom staff in RTÉ, as well as those in the Radio and TV centres, in Presentation and Administration, who have been helpful and supportive. It is easy to be forgetful, particularly as mature years beckon and, after 44 years in journalism, I near retirement and the end of my present career. I say 'present', because I dislike the societal attitude that a human being is useless because a certain age is reached. This is dictated by legislation but not imposed generally, for unilaterally some sectors decree it does not apply to them. I intend to find other means of continuing to contribute to the interest of the maritime sector. I would like to thank all of those who have helped me over the years and who have contributed to *Seascapes* in any way.

It was my father, Sean, who first showed journalistic ability in my family, but the years of the Second World War did not allow for a career as a sports journalist on which he had set his sights. He did contribute a column to the *Evening Echo* in Cork as secretary of the Model Yacht Club, which sailed model yachts on the famous lough in Cork. This is a beautiful location, fed by underground streams, where my wife, Kathleen, and myself used take our young children to feed the swans amongst the wildlife who make their homes there.

To Kathleen, who has stood by me in many changes of home, house, living locations and conditions over the years, who watched as I bought boats that got bigger and bigger and who still reminds me that, when I could neither swim nor sail and we walked as a courting couple on the banks of the River Lee at Blackrock that I used to point at the boats and predict, 'I'll own one some day …' my deep thanks for her encouragement and tolerance. My three sons all took a huge interest in sailing and crewed our boats with me in racing in Cork Harbour and along the south coast, sometimes with agreement, sometimes without.

Sunday evening dinner could be a lively time after winter racing in Cork, when Kathleen and Sinead, my daughter, both of whom prefer sailing in 'nicer conditions' (and there is nothing wrong with that either), would listen to a lively discussion, with items of dinnerware being used to demonstrate who did what, where and when during racing – and who made mistakes!

Kathleen and Sinead, have always been hugely supportive of my work, even when family social occasions were brought to a halt by the ring of a telephone and the urgent demands of RTÉ News. Pat, my eldest son, took to the financial world and sails out of that legendary boating area of Galway, Kinvara. Two of my sons, Cormac and Rowan, took to the sea, both to become master mariners. Captain Cormac has had charge of ships all over the world. Captain Rowan has been deep-sea onboard many types of ships before opting for sail training and the world of tall ships, where he has been mate and captain of *Asgard II*, the national sail training vessel. It was a proud moment for me when I dipped the club ensign at Monkstown Bay in salute to the *Asgard* as he took her upriver past his home place to a berth in Cork City for the first time.

Our expanded family encompasses more in the maritime world. Cormac's wife, our daughter-in-law Sinead Reen, was the first lady in Ireland to qualify as a deck officer and the first to become a master mariner. And the family involvement in the marine sphere continues to spread, as offspring take to the sea, our grandchildren now setting forth on the family boats. Such is the way the maritime world, I hope, will continue to develop as new blood continues to show that this really is an island nation.

SEA ANGLING IN IRELAND
John Rafferty

ISBN: 978 1 85635 553 7

A comprehensive guide to catching the biggest – and best – fish in Irish waters. A must-have for all sea angling enthusiasts, it will also provide invaluable advice to beginners and professionals alike.